SCANDALS OF
THE ROYAL PALACES

SCANDALS OF THE ROYAL PALACES

AN INTIMATE MEMOIR OF ROYALS BEHAVING BADLY

TOM QUINN

Biteback Publishing

First published in Great Britain in 2021 by
Biteback Publishing Ltd, London
Copyright © Tom Quinn 2021

Tom Quinn has asserted his right under the Copyright, Designs and Patents Act 1988
to be identified as the author of this work.

ISBN 978-1-78590-652-7

10 9 8 7 6 5 4 3 2 1

A CIP catalogue record for this book is available from the British Library.

Set in Adobe Caslon Pro

Printed and bound in Great Britain by
CPI Group (UK) Ltd, Croydon CR0 4YY

MIX
Paper from
responsible sources
FSC
www.fsc.org   FSC® C020471

CONTENTS

INTRODUCTION

STRANGE BEDFELLOWS

'Love and scandal are the best sweeteners of tea.'
HENRY FIELDING

George Orwell once said that the British love a really good murder, whether in their novels or their Sunday papers. He might also have said that the only thing the British love more than a good murder is a really good scandal, and best of all are the political and sexual scandals that emanate from Britain's royal palaces.

Of course, the kiss and tell story is now a commonplace, but scandal itself isn't a recent phenomenon. It has a long history; one tied up with power and position, especially royal power and royal position; a history that includes scandals in such high places so damaging – Edward and Mrs Simpson's relationship, for example – that when they do blow up, they become lodged in the collective consciousness never to be forgotten.

But dozens of other royal scandals have been covered up or

suppressed to some degree by an establishment that is famous for its determination to keep royal secrets, well, secret.

This book is the first in-depth look at the outrageous behaviour of not just the royals themselves but also palace officials, courtiers, household servants and hangers-on. Covering existing royal palaces in some depth as well as taking a briefer look at scandals linked to long-vanished royal residences such as Whitehall, Nonsuch and Kings Langley, *Scandals of the Royal Palaces* also includes new information on well-known and not-so-well-known scandals, including those that have only recently been revealed in detail through the release of previously secret official papers.

Political, social, financial and sexual scandals have been linked to Britain's royal palaces for centuries – from Edward II potentially being killed because of his attraction to men to drug-fuelled and lesbian queens, perjurers, liars, thieves and even Nazi sympathisers, the royal residences have seen it all.

The behaviour of today's royals seems perpetually to threaten scandal; three of HRH Queen Elizabeth's children are divorced following adulterous affairs and one was the friend of a notorious paedophile. Meanwhile, the two sons of the Prince of Wales – himself no stranger to scandal – have publicly fallen out with the press and with each other.

As this book will show, scandal and the royal family have always been strange and not-so-strange bedfellows, and key to the sometimes extraordinary scandals the royals have become involved in are the palaces in which they live. Free to move between some of the most luxurious homes in England – Windsor

Castle, Kensington Palace, Balmoral and Buckingham Palace, to name but four – and living in a world of excessive deference and financial security, members of the royal family find it impossible to resist the lure of flattery and personal power. Since they are often unhappy in their gilded cages it is perhaps no wonder that down the ages royal men and women have used their position and influence to get what they want – whether that be sex, drugs or money – while hoping to maintain their reputations as moral leaders.

Readers may ask, why a book about royal scandals, many of which are already well known? First, new information is always becoming available. Second, interpretations and our under-standing of the past change as society changes. We are far more accepting of same-sex relationships today, for example, than we ever were in the past. We are also far less deferential to the royal family. Even fifty years ago biographers of members of the royal family tended to gloss over their subjects' sexual peccadilloes.

Few today would think it a good thing always to suppress the misdeeds of royal individuals just because they happen to be royal. The sense that we are all equal is far stronger now than it was historically when the sole aim of the establishment was to protect the reputation of public figures by whatever means necessary. Where biographers and historians in the past felt their role was to uphold the dignity of members of the royal family by suppressing anything deemed to be damaging to their reputations, we now see that a warts-and-all picture is far more accurate and interesting.

The truth is that we have come a long way – so far, indeed,

that in 2018 the royal family happily announced the marriage between Ivar Mountbatten, a cousin of the Queen, and his partner James Coyle. Perhaps what makes this even more extraordinary – and further evidence of just how far we have come in our attitudes and values – is that Ivar's former wife, Penny Mountbatten, gave her ex-husband away.

The world is a healthier place since the death of Earl Mountbatten of Burma, Ivar's ancestor, who spent his life concealing from the public and his friends his promiscuous taste for young men; a taste he was happy to indulge to an extraordinary degree safe in the knowledge that no newspaper would ever print anything he did not like.

We live in an age of far greater freedom; freedom to discuss the lives, loves and indiscretions of the most famous family in the world, a family whose members – as we will see – have intrigued and embarrassed, outraged and entranced us for centuries.

CHAPTER ONE

THE KING AND
HIS HUSBAND

'Is it not strange that he is thus bewitched?'
CHRISTOPHER MARLOWE, *EDWARD II*

Visitors to London are sometimes confused by the fact that the British Parliament meets in the Palace of Westminster, a building that is obviously not a palace at all. In fact, the name has survived where the palace, in the sense of a royal residence, has not. We know that the late Saxon kings including Cnut and Edward the Confessor lived in a palace where the 'palace' of Westminster now stands. The area was once known as Thorney Island, a marshy area, criss-crossed by streams and surrounded by mudflats but which lay at an important and strategic crossing point on the River Thames. Edward the Confessor built the first palace there. He also built, probably simultaneously, the great minster or church – Westminster Abbey – which still stands, though much altered, today.

It is difficult today to visualise the very early palace because over succeeding centuries it gradually expanded until it sprawled from the river across almost to St James's Park in one direction and from the Jewel Tower, which still exists, to Charing Cross in the other. The palace eventually surrounded the abbey itself and continued past the Jewel Tower to what is now Great College Street. Beyond the outer wall, which followed the route of modern Great College Street, was a narrow path and a water-filled ditch, the remains of which were discovered during work in the 1970s.

The fact that the minster and the palace were almost coterminous in this early period simply reflects the closeness between the king and the church, between temporal and spiritual power. And it was to the old palace at Westminster that the King's Council (the *Curia Regis*), the forerunner of Parliament, was summoned whenever the king felt it was necessary. Nothing remains of the buildings from the time of Edward the Confessor or indeed from the time of William I, but William II's magnificent Westminster Hall still exists and it was there that the king met his council. Of course, during the medieval period, the king tended to move almost continually around the country and ministers and advisers would follow him, but the Palace of Westminster along with the Tower of London were his London residences.

By modern standards, the old medieval palace would have seemed sparsely furnished with simple wooden furniture and chests but also rich fabric hangings dyed in surprisingly bright colours. Visitors to the meticulously restored rooms at the Tower of London can get a more accurate idea of what the king's apartments at Westminster might have looked like. But we should remember that important items, such as the king's bed, were deliberately made in such a way that they could easily be dismantled to be carried with the king on his never-ending journeys around the country.

By the time of Edward II (1284–1327), the earls who had formed the *Curia Regis* had been joined by representatives of the towns and boroughs across England. This Model Parliament, as it was known, had been introduced in 1295 under Edward I and arguably began a long process of democratisation which continues to this day with attempts to remove hereditary peers from the House of Lords.

These early Parliaments were not recognisably Parliaments in the modern sense. They met irregularly, usually when the king needed money. In return for Parliament agreeing to introduce taxes to pay for the king's wars, the king agreed to listen to the grievances and petitions of his more important subjects.

But although the old Palace of Westminster looms large in the popular imagination as the setting for many of the most tumultuous scenes of Edward II's extraordinary life, he actually spent a great deal more time at his palace at Kings Langley in Hertfordshire, of which not a trace survives today.

* * *

The modern village of Kings Langley is twenty-one miles from the Palace of Westminster. It gets its name from the palace built there, on lands formerly owned by the Abbey of St Albans but acquired by Eleanor of Castile, wife of Edward I, in 1276. Work on the palace, which was situated at the top of a hill to the west of the village, probably began shortly thereafter. By 1308, a year after Edward II's coronation, a Dominican priory had been established next to the new palace – here as elsewhere it was important that king and church should seem almost coterminous.

Surviving records from 1291–92 reveal that the great hall at Kings Langley was decorated with 'fifty-four shields and a picture of four knights seeking a tournament'. The palace included private apartments for the king and queen, which would have looked much like the recreated royal apartments we see at the Tower of London today.

Though he was born hundreds of miles away at Caernarfon Castle, Edward II spent most of his early years at Kings Langley and it was always his favourite palace. It was also to be the final resting place of the man for whom he was forced to give up his throne.

According to the Kings Langley History Society, the palace included:

> three courts. The great court contained the principal royal apartments which included the hall and chapel, prince's chamber and queen's chamber. The domestic buildings [included a] bakery, larder, roasting house and saucery in addition to the Great Kitchen. There were also stables, barns and mills, a hunting lodge and Great and Little Parks and gardens.

Through the reigns of Edward III and Richard II, the palace

was repaired and expanded. But its associations with Edward II and with the ill-fated Richard II, murdered at Pontefract and initially buried at Kings Langley, may have made the place seemed cursed, for by the time of Henry VIII, the palace had fallen into near-ruin.

Today, though the site is officially listed as an ancient monument, nothing remains of the palace. But as the wind blows across the open hilltop, it is easy to imagine Edward arriving with his favourite, Piers Gaveston (c.1284–1312), through the thick woodland that once covered the area.

* * *

Despite their fame, or in some cases infamy, we know relatively little about the personal lives of English medieval kings. The Plantagenets ruled England from 1154 to 1485 and we know a great deal about their wars, their marriages and indeed about the great constitutional changes, such as Magna Carta, that occurred during their reigns, but the details of their private passions are more difficult to trace. There is, however, an exception – Edward II.

The story of Piers Gaveston and Edward II has been told so often but historians take different, sometimes vehemently opposing, views about what really went on between the two men. As recently as the 1960s, authors tended to skirt over the issue of whether or not Edward's relationship with Gaveston was physical. This was a reflection not of the existence or otherwise of evidence about a physical relationship; it was evidence that, even in the 1960s, homosexuality was still a subject many people felt it was improper even to discuss.

Members of the royal family were known to have been gay or bisexual – Elizabeth II's great-uncle Albert, for example – but it was not done to write about these things or to expose someone unless they were so indiscreet that exposure and condemnation became inevitable. Homosexuality was a fact of life, especially aristocratic life; everyone was aware of it, but the point was not to discuss it and not to get caught. Hypocrisy did not matter. The MPs Jeremy Thorpe and Tom Driberg, later Baron Bradwell, are good examples. Both were prominent public figures – Thorpe an Old Etonian and rising political star, Driberg a peer – yet both were able to continue their respectable lives despite their friends' and colleagues' full awareness that they were behaving in ways that, at the time, were criminal. Driberg got away with it. Thorpe was not so lucky; having become embroiled in numerous gay affairs, his life fell apart when he was accused of having conspired to murder a troublesome former lover. Thorpe and Driberg, though influential establishment figures, still had to seem to be obeying the rules or at least not get caught disobeying them. Not so for monarchs in late medieval England. Their lives were lived in the public arena, an arena in which keeping secrets was all but impossible.

* * *

Born on 25 April 1284, Edward II was just twenty-three when his father died and he became king. As the fourth son of Edward I, he was never destined for the throne; but for the deaths of his older brothers, he might have lived in relative obscurity.

From the start, his reign was characterised by personal, political and military difficulties that he seemed ill-equipped to deal with. Within months of becoming king, Edward had invested Gaveston, a Gascon nobleman, with the title Earl of Cornwall. Edward's older advisers whose titles were far more ancient were incensed. The situation grew worse almost daily as a man seen as an upstart became the centre of Edward's public and private life. Gaveston was given jewels, money, land and titles at such a pace and in such an extravagant fashion that rumours began to spread that the two men were lovers.

It is easy to dismiss this as an accusation invented long after Edward's death simply to further blacken the name of a man who was seen for many reasons as a failed king. Over time, the stories of successful monarchs tend to be embellished so that it can seem as if they could do no wrong; over time, failed kings become ever more useless, ever more monstrous. This was true, for example, of Richard II, deposed for sheer incompetence, and Richard III, defeated at Bosworth by Henry Tudor but not before he had apparently murdered the princes in the Tower of London.

The truth about Edward II is that he failed to understand that although he was a monarch with the right to rule as he chose, he could not survive without the support of the group of aristocrats just below him in the ranks of the powerful. These aristocrats – the so-called barons – didn't mind what Edward did to those below them, but they saw their own privileges as sacrosanct regardless of the power of the king. Which is why, in 1311, some twenty-one of the great landowning noblemen drew up a document known as the Ordinances.

One of the first written attempts to restrict the powers of the monarch, the Ordinances focused mainly on financial matters and aimed to remove the right of the king to appoint whomever he liked without consultation. Clearly, both these areas of the king's power related directly to the manner in which Edward had appointed and promoted Piers Gaveston. Having agreed to the terms of the Ordinances, Edward seems to have realised that the forces ranged against him were too formidable to resist and he also agreed to Gaveston's banishment. This was, as it were, merely a tactical retreat and by 1313, Gaveston was back in England. The great landowning earls had had enough. Gaveston was kidnapped and quickly executed by the second most powerful man in the land, Edward's cousin Thomas, Earl of Lancaster.

Around this time Edward's personal difficulties were made worse by the rebellion of Robert the Bruce in Scotland. Edward's army met the Bruce army at Bannockburn in 1314 and Edward was defeated. Had he won this decisive battle, his personal history might have been very different – a great military leader could arguably do as he pleased; a military failure could not. Certainly, Edward's reputation would have been enhanced rather than fatally damaged. With Edward's loss of Scotland – a loss blamed personally on him – the Earl of Lancaster began to behave as if he were the king or at least the king of northern England.

So, on the one side we have Edward, still raging over the death of his favourite, and on the other is the Earl of Lancaster, who is now Edward's bitter enemy. A third group of earls led by Aymer De Valence tried to make peace between the two factions.

*   *   *

Edward's need for male favourites seems at this time almost pathological. With Gaveston out of the way, Edward might have focused his attention on his political difficulties, especially with regard to Scotland. Instead, he was soon obsessing about a new male favourite, or rather two male favourites: Hugh le Despenser (1261–1326) and his son, also Hugh (c.1287–1326). They became replacements for the lost Gaveston.

Despenser the Elder, later the Earl of Winchester, had been a friend and adviser to Edward's father and was one of a small number of barons who had supported Edward II in the row over Gaveston. Despenser the Younger had actually supported the barons in their claims against Gaveston and their insistence that he be exiled. But the shifting sands of politics and personal favouritism soon brought him close to Edward and in a pattern that parallels remarkably closely the king's behaviour towards Gaveston, the Despensers began to receive numerous gifts and honours. Though the younger Despenser was seen as the more corrupt, his father also became the focus of huge resentment.

At this distance in time, it seems extraordinary that the Despensers, both father and son, could not see the dangers of becoming Edward's favourites. By accepting the king's extravagant gifts – including castles, titles and vast estates in Wales

and elsewhere – father and son were always going to be accused of corruption, while the king would be accused of lack of
judgement.

Inevitably, Edward's obsession with his new favourites led to
rebellion. The barons insisted the Despensers be exiled and they
left England in 1321, less than a decade after Gaveston's execution. But in an act of almost suicidal stupidity and to the fury of
Edward's wife Isabella (c.1295 –1358), Thomas of Lancaster and
other barons, the king allowed the Despensers to return to England barely a year later.

Rebellion led to war and Edward's army met the defiant
Thomas of Lancaster at Boroughbridge in Yorkshire in 1322.
Lancaster was defeated and executed by Edward – an act widely
seen as revenge for Gaveston's death.

Unable to learn from his own past mistakes, Edward continued to reward the Despensers with gifts and titles. He formally
revoked the Ordinances and seemed to lose any sense that he
might be making enemies. His own queen eventually lost pa-
tience and while on a diplomatic mission to Paris in 1325, Isabella switched sides and became the mistress of one of Edward's
greatest enemies, Roger Mortimer, a man who had gone into
exile to avoid the same fate as Thomas of Lancaster.

A year later Mortimer invaded England with the full sup-
port of Isabella, defeated Edward and executed the Despensers.
Edward was forced to abdicate and his son became Edward III.
For centuries it was believed that Edward II was murdered in
Berkeley Castle in 1327, but there is some evidence to suggest he

survived until 1330 after secretly leaving England. This theory is based on a letter written by Italian bishop Manuele Fieschi to Edward III and discovered in an old archive in the 1880s. Fieschi claims Edward escaped abroad after 1327 and, although there is little additional evidence to support the claim, it has the support of a number of historians.

Curiously given her role in deposing her own husband, Isabella insisted on being buried with Edward II's heart and wearing the mantle she had worn when she married him – acts hardly suggestive of a hatred for her husband.

*   *   *

When Edward was born, no one imagined that later in life he would be engulfed in scandal, but from the perspective of the twenty-first century it becomes clearer that the warning signs were there from very early on. From his teenage years and long before Gaveston became an issue, Edward broke the rules. It was almost as if he needed to live dangerously or needed constantly to provoke those around him unless he favoured them personally. He was a creature of extremes: if he hated a man, he was known to be vengeful; if he favoured someone, he would hear nothing against them.

Contemporaneous chronicles describe the young Edward as tall, good looking and immensely strong. He might, on the face of it, have been just the sort of king his contemporaries would have most admired – after all, this was an age in which kings were still expected to show personal strength and bravery. It was unthinkable that a king should choose not to personally lead his troops in battle.

Although he was routed by Robert the Bruce – a serious black mark against him – Edward did defeat his cousin Thomas of Lancaster at Boroughbridge and there is no contemporaneous suggestion that he was anything other than physically brave.

The great scandal of Edward's youth was that his strength and physical prowess were directed in ways seen as disgraceful and demeaning: he loved music and dancing, which was just about acceptable, but he also developed a taste for physical activities that astonished those around him.

According to *The Chronicle of Lanercost*, an anonymous Latin history of England and Scotland covering the years 1201–1346 and probably written or compiled at Lanercost Priory in Cumbia, Edward's private enthusiasms included hedging and ditching, rowing, bricklaying, cart driving, thatching and shoeing horses. These were the occupations of peasants and it was unseemly and undignified for a king even to notice such occupations let alone take part in them. Edward's contemporaries would undoubtedly have agreed with Sir Walter Raleigh who singled out only one activity at which a king needed to excel: 'There is no art or other knowledge so seemly or necessary for a prince, as the art military.'

Even today there is an echo of this tradition in the royal family. Elizabeth II's three sons all spent some time doing military service, as did her grandsons William and Harry, and if one looks at certain regiments (the Brigade of Guards and the Royal

Green Jackets, for example), it is easy to find officers from very grand landed families who speak of 'the profession of arms' in a way that Sir Walter Raleigh and monarchs of earlier ages would have understood.

Just as there were punishments for peasants who behaved in ways that were inappropriate to their station in life, so there were punishments for members of the nobility who behaved in ways that were seen as demeaning to their status. Edward's demeaning behaviour was a problem not just because it reflected badly on him as an individual king but because it reflected badly on the institution of the monarchy.

It is difficult to appreciate today the extent to which the medieval court was a public arena. Indeed, the idea of privacy in the modern sense did not exist at this time – the Latin root of the word 'privacy' suggests not a comfortable quiet time with friends and family but instead isolation and the absence of others, a meaning that survives in the word 'privation'.

There is also the importance of form; noblemen stood intensely on their dignity. Servants who showed disrespect to their lord could and probably would be killed. Any perceived slight might bring a violent physical response – knights might go to war with each other over such things. In 1609, for example, Sir George Wharton and Sir James Stewart, who had been great friends up to this point, fell out over a game of cards. They fought a duel the next day in Islington fields and both were killed. The question of honour (which still plagues many parts of the world today) survived into the nineteenth century when two gentlemen would fire pistols at each other from point-blank range if they felt their honour had been impugned. Medieval noblemen were far more sensitive to these things, even if the perceived lack of respect emanated from a king.

Edward had been made Prince of Wales in 1301 – indeed, he was the first of that title – and presumably at this stage, since he was not yet king, the nobles would have felt able to tolerate his eccentricities. They probably assumed, wrongly as it turned out, that he would grow out of these absurd lowly interests and adopt the proper pursuits of the nobility: hunting, jousting and war. But this was not to be.

Our source for much of Edward's life is *The Chronicle of Walter of Guisborough*, first published in 1687. We know very little about Guisborough, but he was almost certainly a canon at Guisborough Priory in Yorkshire and though his account of Edward's reign may be based on earlier, now lost, accounts by others, it fits a general picture of a man at loggerheads with his family and his duty and with what was expected of him. Indeed, if the Guisborough chronicle is to be believed, Edward seems to have been an early example of what looks very much like teenage rebellion. He was certainly what biographer Kathryn Warner calls 'the unconventional king' and this unconventionality was perceived both then and in the centuries that followed his death as scandalous.

* * *

The great question about Edward is simply this: was his relationship with Piers Gaveston, and later on with the younger

Despenser, simply a question of friendship, the bond of brothers who just happened to get along wonderfully well, or were these relationships a combination of intense affection combined with physical love? In other words, did this deeply unconventional king have a same-sex relationship with Gaveston at least if not Despenser?

Recent biographers have taken opposing views. In his *Edward II the Man: A Doomed Inheritance*, Stephen Spinks argues that Edward did indeed have a physical relationship with Gaveston. By contrast, California State University academic Jochen Burgtorf believes the two men were simply platonic friends. Kathryn Warner, in her book *Edward II: The Unconventional King*, takes a middle view and thinks we will simply never know for sure. The only direct, unequivocal evidence that Gaveston and Edward were lovers comes from Jean Froissart's *Chronicles*, which were written long after Edward's death, probably in the last quarter of the fourteenth century. Froissart himself was not born until 1337 and we know that much of his material, like that of Walter of Guisborough, was copied from earlier sources. With these caveats in mind, we must approach Froissart with caution, but he is unequivocal in his description of the relationship between Gaveston and Edward as 'sodomitic'. Against this we must weigh the fact that by the time Froissart was writing his chronicles, the conventional judgement of Edward had become fixed: he had failed as a king and must therefore be guilty of every possible sin.

Even allowing for differences of opinion among professional scholars and uncertain historical evidence, one thing remains both true and remarkable: Edward's friendship with his male favourite was intense and passionate. Stephen Spinks sums the situation up neatly: 'While no evidence explicitly states that they were lovers, the action and policies of the king … give a clear indication as to motivation.' Spinks continues: 'The act of same-sex intimacy was not tolerated. However, Edward was a king and his position allowed him the freedom to express his intimate attachment to Gaveston in ways that many at the time were not able to do.'

Edward's rational side – the side that told him his very position as king might be threatened if he pursued his passion for Gaveston – was overthrown by what can be described only as a passion that must have included a physical element. It is a situation that has many parallels in recent times – the brilliant parliamentarian Jeremy Thorpe, for example, threw all rational considerations aside in his passion for Norman Scott. Thorpe took terrible risks with his career and his public standing by sending passionate letters on House of Commons notepaper to both Scott and dozens of other male lovers at a time when homosexual acts represented a serious criminal offence. Despite the enormous value he put on his career, Thorpe, like Edward II, could do no other than respond to a passion that almost always overrode sense and reason – and it was the physical element of this passion that was key to its excessive nature. Likewise, Edward simply could not stop himself loading Gaveston down with land, titles, jewels and money – objective manifestations of the extent of his passion. Had he and Gaveston simply been friends, the advice and warnings of powerful men across England would surely not have been ignored and though Edward might still have ennobled his friend and even made him rich, he would not, perhaps, have ignored at his peril the code that governed the behaviour of kings and noblemen.

Edward's greatest act of folly given the standards of the time was to leave Gaveston as Regent of England during the king's absence in France in 1308. It is difficult to believe that Edward had no idea that he would enrage his advisers by this act. Most of the powerful men who surrounded Edward had every reason to resent taking orders, however temporarily, from a young Frenchman from an obscure family. They knew that according to the rules, one of them should have been made Regent in Edward's absence. Breaking this rule simply told the barons that Edward was either mad or bad or both: in short, he was not fit to be king.

* * *

Although Froissart's reference to a 'sodomitic' relationship dates from long after Edward and Gaveston had died, there were contemporaneous references that went almost as far. The anonymous author of the *Annales Paulini 1307–1340*, for example, writes under the entry for 1308 that Edward's love for Gaveston was 'beyond measure'.

Power and sexual desire combined are especially corrupting on a personal as well as a political level, which explains why the powerful have always used their position to extract favours, especially sexual favours, from lesser mortals.

By 1577, the year Raphael Holinshed's *Chronicles of England, Scotland and Ireland* were published, historians were simply repeating and embellishing tales about Edward that had been handed down for centuries and in an age when something written down in a previous century had the authority bestowed by long use, Edward's name was increasingly blackened. Soon nothing good could be said about him as either a king or a man.

The modern idea of looking for historical evidence to back up statements of fact was still a long way off and chroniclers simply repeated what had always been said. Holinshed writes:

But now concerning the demeanour of this new king, whose disordered manners brought himself and many others unto destruction; we find that in the beginning of his government, though he was of nature given to lightness, yet being restrained with the prudent advertisements of certain of his councillors, to the end that he might shew some likelihood of good proof, he counterfeited a kind of gravity, vertue and modesty; but yet he could not thoroughly be so bridled, but that forthwith he began to play divers wanton and light parts, at the first indeed not outrageously, but by little and little, and that covertly. For having revoked again into England his old mate the said Piers de Gaveston, he received him into most high favour, creating him Earl of Cornwall, and Lord of Man, his principal secretary, and Lord Chamberlain of the realm, through whose company and society he was suddenly so corrupted, that he burst out into most heinous vices; for then using the said Piers as a procurer of his disordered doings, he began to have his nobles in no regard, to set nothing by their instructions, and to take small heed unto the good government of the commonwealth, so that within a while, he gave himself to wantonness, passing his time in voluptuous pleasure, and riotous excess: and to help them forward in that kind of life, the foresaid Piers, who (as it may be thought, he had sworn to make the king to forget himself, and the state, to the which he was called) furnished his court with companies of jesters, ruffians, flattering parasites, musicians, and other vile and naughty ribalds, that the king might spend both days and nights in jesting, playing, blanketing, and in such other filthy and dishonourable exercises: and moreover, desirous to advance those that were like to him self, he procured for them honourable offices, all which notable preferments and dignities, since they were ill bestowed, were rather to be accounted dishonourable than otherwise.

The references to 'most heinous vices' and 'filthy and dishonourable exercises' are as close as Holinshed gets to specifying the accusation of sodomy levelled at Edward. Froissart as we have seen was far more direct in his accusation of sexual impropriety. Christopher Marlowe's famous play *Edward II* was published in 1594 and is damning, but playwrights are notorious for embellishing for dramatic purposes. That Edward's flaws were fixed for ever in the public mind can also be seen in succeeding generations. In *A Chronicle of the Kings of England*, published in 1643, Richard Baker writes: 'Never did a prince come to a crown with more applause of nobility and people ... yet seldom doth advancement in honour alter men to the better; to the worse often and commonly then when it is joined with an authority that sets them above controlment.'

That is the key to Edward's problem: he was, or felt he was, above 'controlment'.

For Baker, the barons had no choice but to take matters into their own hands:

[Gaveston] now made the king not only more vicious than he would otherwise have been, but vicious where otherwise he would not have been; and therefore great cause in regard of the king, to remove Gaveston from his company; and no less in regard to the lords themselves; for Gaveston advancing was their debasing; his greatness with the king made them but ciphers; but in regard to the common-wealth most cause of all; for while the king was altogether ruled by Gaveston and Gaveston himself was altogether irregular, the common-wealth could have but little hope of justice; but was sure to suffer as long as Gaveston was suffered.

But Baker does at least acknowledge Edward's good points: 'He was fair of body and of great strength ... he was extreme in nothing but loving ... he was rather unfortunate than unhappy ... two vertues were eminent in him above all his predecessors, continence and abstinence: so continent that he left no base issue behind him.'

Not leaving any illegitimate children might seem a virtue but this was unusual and it may well be a back-handed compliment as kings were almost expected to show their virility by having mistresses and making them pregnant. Could it be that having fulfilled his dynastic duty by having heirs with his wife he did not need to have a mistress since mistresses were about pleasure and Edward sought his pleasure with Gaveston?

* * *

By the nineteenth century, historians tended to be more euphemistic about exactly what Edward was accused of – British Victorian writers could not bring themselves to write unambiguously about a subject so far beyond the pale as homosexuality. It was only in the second half of the twentieth century that writers felt able to discuss in an open and honest manner whether or not Edward II was gay or at least bisexual. The latter seems to be the current view. Certainly, like all medieval kings, Edward saw marriage as a purely political and dynastic necessity. In modern times such 'lavender' marriages – between a man and a woman whereby one or both of them are predominantly or exclusively gay – were and no doubt still are commonplace. The past century is littered with examples of politicians and members of the royal family who knew that in order to conform and be successful, they needed to be married and preferably have children. Becoming Prime Minister was for a long time seen as virtually impossible if you happened to be a single man – Edward Heath is a rare exception but he was plagued by rumours about his sexuality, rumours that damaged his effectiveness as Prime Minister.

Rumours during his lifetime also plagued Edward II's reign and those rumours continued and were made more lurid in the centuries after his death, blinding historians – until recently – to the real merits and demerits of his rule.

The truth is that the loss of Scotland to Robert the Bruce probably did more to blacken Edward's historical reputation as an effective king than his hedging and ditching and even his relationship with Gaveston.

Scandal is rather like a snowball – once in motion, it picks up mass and momentum until it becomes unstoppable and, whatever the objective truth, even assuming such truth could be unearthed, members of the royal family whose reputations are badly damaged can be sure of one thing: they are very rarely rehabilitated.

CHAPTER TWO

TRACES REMAIN: PALACES RISE AND FALL

*'Nothing but a heap of Houses, erected at divers times, and of
different Models, which they made Contiguous in the best Manner
they could for the Residence of the Court...'*
SAMUEL DE SORBIÈRE (1615–70) ON WHITEHALL

I t is perhaps worth taking a brief pause at this point to look at
the monarch's two most important London residences in this
early period; key locations where Edward II and later kings and
queens spent their days discussing affairs of state, meeting their
ministers and friends and gossiping and intriguing.

During the tumultuous years of Edward's love-tortured reign,
he spent much of his time as we have seen at Kings Langley,
the palace where as the Prince of Wales he had been allowed to
indulge his love of manual labour. While in London, Edward
lived at the old Palace of Westminster, completed in 1099, or
the Tower of London. Of the old Palace of Westminster, only
Westminster Hall and the Jewel Tower still survive, and it was at

Westminster Hall, its interior then brightly painted, that much of the business of government – including angry scenes between the barons and Edward and Gaveston – would have played out.

Much of the old Palace of Westminster burned down in 1512. Henry VIII (1491–1547), needing another palace nearby, looked jealously to the west of his fire-ravaged residence. And when he looked west, Henry saw where Cardinal Thomas Wolsey, referred to at the time as second in wealth and power only to the king, lived at York Place, the London residence of the archbishops of York. York Place was situated towards the Trafalgar Square end of modern Whitehall. Wolsey, who among his numerous titles was also the Archbishop of York, had expanded and enriched York Place to reflect his own importance, but this was a dangerous game to play and when Wolsey failed to persuade the Pope to annul the king's marriage to Catherine of Aragon, Henry accused him of treachery. This was a standard ploy for Henry when someone had displeased him and everyone knew it was politically motivated, but that did not lessen the effect of the accusation. By 1530 Wolsey had been removed from all his offices and Henry conveniently helped himself to York Place.

Many of the structures that made up York Place were built from white stone and as a result, by the early 1530s, the king's new residence had earned itself a nickname: Whitehall. In succeeding centuries, it was to expand piecemeal until the Palace of Whitehall covered an astonishing seventy-three acres and boasted more than 1,500 rooms, but it was a mishmash of styles with no coherent overall architectural principle. Its labyrinthine layout – it took months, apparently, for new residents to find their way around – meant that for James I and Charles II it provided a perfect setting for their scandalous private lives.

At the end of the seventeenth century Edward Hatton (c.1664–1733) describes the importance of Whitehall compared with other royal residences:

> Heretofore there have been many courts of our kings and queens in London and Westminster, as the Tower of London, where some believe Julius Cæsar lodged, and William the Conqueror; in the Old Jewry, where Henry VI.; Baynard's Castle, where Henry VII.; Bridewell, where John and Henry VIII.; Tower Royal, where Richard II. and Stephen; the Wardrobe, in Great Carter Lane, where Richard III. [resided]; also at Somerset House, kept by Queen Elizabeth, and at Westminster, near the Hall, where Edward the Confessor, and several other kings, kept their courts. But of later times the place for the Court, when in town, was mostly Whitehall, a very pleasant and commodious situation, looking into St James's Park, the canal, &c., on the west, and the noble river of Thames on the east; Privy Garden, with fountain, statues, &c., and an open prospect to the statue at Charing Cross on the north.

It is difficult now to appreciate the extent and variety of the Palace of Whitehall – it was almost completely destroyed by another fire in 1698 – but if one imagines a mix of St James's Palace and Hampton Court Palace, combined perhaps with Knole House in Kent, one would have a fair idea of that long-vanished architectural oddity.

Added to the mix of courtyards, alleys and jumbled houses that made up the old palace, there was a jousting area, a cock pit, a bowling green, tennis courts, riverside walks and formal gardens. All that survives today of the later palace (other than Westminster Hall and the Jewel Tower) is the Banqueting Hall of 1622, so a late addition, but cleaned and seen in the sparkling light of a mid-summer's day, its pale stone still gives us a glimpse of what the old Palace of Whitehall must have been like.

Edward II and other medieval monarchs spent far less time at the Tower of London, largely because it had developed into more of a fortress than a sumptuous home even at this early period. But the Tower still held enormous symbolic power, which is why, for example, Edward VI, Mary I and Elizabeth I spent a night or two there before their coronations.

In *Old and New London* published in 1878, Walter Thornbury confirms this shift in the Tower's role as a royal residence:

> From and after the reign of Elizabeth the Court no longer oscil-lated between Greenwich, the Tower, and Westminster, moving about the goods and chattels of the Crown as occasion served. Though the Tower was still theoretically the seat of all the great attributes of royalty, and was sometimes occupied by the sover-eign upon occasions of extraordinary solemnity, yet, from this time forth, Whitehall became the settled and fixed centre of courtly splendour and magnificence.

Strictly speaking, the medieval palace at the Tower of London was confined to three towers, all of which have survived, though they have been partly or completely rebuilt. St Thomas's Tower was built by Edward I in the 1270s and the Wakefield and Lanthorn Towers in the first quarter of the same century. The queen's apartments were probably in the Lanthorn Tower, while the king's apartments were in the Wakefield and St Thomas's Towers.

The curious thing about the Tower of London is that its enormous significance as a symbol of power had so little to do with its role as a place where the monarch might actually live. Its spartan, garrison-like qualities may have meant a great deal in the centuries after the Norman conquest when kings were still expected to be warriors, but as time passed more luxurious residences began to exert an irresistible pull on monarchs concerned more with the majesty of their appearance and surroundings.

CHAPTER THREE

SWEET CHILD AND WIFE: THE FORBIDDEN LOVES OF JAMES I

'All kings is mostly rapscallions...'

MARK TWAIN, *THE ADVENTURES OF HUCKLEBERRY FINN*

Between the death of Edward II in 1327 and the accession of James I (1566–1625) to the English throne in 1603, there were of course many scandalous monarchs – Richard III, widely believed to have murdered the princes in the Tower of London, and wife-killer Henry VIII to name but two – but their bad behaviour was perceived as a matter of strength rather than hidden weakness. Violent arbitrary kings were as often as not admired. Not so kings who indulged a taste for handsome young men.

The need for monarchs and princes to seem ruthless and warlike was almost taken for granted. As late as 1743, during the War of the Austrian Succession, George II led his troops into battle. Even queens felt the need to emphasise their soldierly qualities

– Elizabeth I, though prevented from fighting due to her sex, made her famous speech at Tilbury in 1588 saying, 'I may have the body of a weak and feeble woman, but I have the heart and stomach of a king.' More significantly, if theatrically, she was dressed carefully and deliberately in armour and mounted on a war horse. In the late sixteenth and early seventeenth centuries, a succession of monarchs read Polydore Vergil's *Anglica Historia* (published in 1534). Here queens and kings were told to 'seek fame by military skill'.

We have seen how Edward II's courage in battle was not questioned, despite losing at Bannockburn, but this was not enough to outweigh the scandal of his love for another man. More than two centuries after his death, another monarch struggled to maintain his martial and kingly dignity in the face of a scandal involving not one but several young male favourites.

Sir Anthony Weldon, in his *The Court and Character of King James* published in 1651, wrote: 'he [James I of England and VI of Scotland] was the most cowardly man that I ever knew'. Though Weldon was writing after James's death, they were roughly contemporaries. Weldon's judgement undoubtedly has more to do with the scandals surrounding James's private life than with his military prowess; after all, James had fought on at least six occasions before leaving Scotland to accept the English throne in 1603.

So, it is no surprise that James is depicted wearing heavy armour in Rubens's great ceiling painting at the remnant of the old Palace of Westminster, the Banqueting House.

But, as with Edward II, no amount of bravery on the battle-field, essential though that was, could outweigh the scandal of James's taste for young men, a taste that almost certainly included dangerous and highly scandalous physical relationships with several of the young aristocrats he found irresistible. Unlike Edward, James had the political nous to keep his dangerous love for various young men largely separate from his role as king. He was a defender of the notion of the absolute and divine right of kings but he combined this with a practical acceptance of the realities of English politics. He knew that it was dangerous to alienate powerful nobles. He may have been indiscreet – something which damaged his reputation in the long run – but he kept his throne because at least compared with Edward II, he was politically astute.

James wrote often to the men who inspired his most intense feelings and these letters survive. As David Bergeron explains in *King James and Letters of Homoerotic Desire*, 'The inscription that moves across the letters spells desire.'

It may be that James's first intimate relationship, which occurred when he was still a child, was so intense that it induced a desire in him to repeat the experience as often as he could in adulthood. He was just thirteen when he met Esmé Stewart (1542–1583). Stewart was thirty-seven and their relationship almost immediately caused alarm throughout the court.

An English visitor Sir Henry Widdrington confided to a friend: 'The King altogether is persuaded and led by him [Stewart] … and is in such love with him as in the open sight of the people often he will clasp him about the neck with his arms and kiss him.'

Widdrington's reflections suggest a king who was continually prone to falling in love with young men: 'It is thowght this Kinge is to[o] muche caryed by yonge men that lyes in his chamber and is his mynions.' And Stewart was not the only courtier treated in this way. The Earl of Huntly was also a favourite. Widdrington describes how James 'kissed him at times to the amazement of many'.

In a drama that has almost uncanny parallels with Edward and Gaveston, James was reckless in his desire to please his friend. Stewart was created Lord Darnley and the Earl of Lennox and was given priceless jewels from James's mother Mary Queen of Scots's collection, including a chain of rubies and diamonds known as the Great Harry.

But Stewart was a Catholic and this fact combined with what was seen by many as his corrupt manipulation of James turned the Scottish nobles against him. Unlike Gaveston, Stewart tried to avoid unduly antagonising the nobles – he even agreed to renounce his Catholicism. But they were not convinced that his conversion to Protestantism was genuine and in 1582 a proclamation was issued which accused Stewart of being involved in the murder of James's father Lord Darnley and others. He was also accused of 'international intrigues'. Forced into exile in France, Stewart kept up a secret correspondence with James, a correspondence that lasted until Stewart's death in 1583.

One of the underlying justifications for the nobles' insistence that Stewart be exiled was that he was seen as having exerted too much control over the royal household. But for the dour Calvinists surrounding James, there was a deeper unease, centred on something they could hardly bear to contemplate.

Unlike Edward, James did not dare bring his favourite back from France and in fact they were never to meet again.

Any doubts about the love between the two men can be dismissed as Stewart left instructions that after his death his heart should be sealed in a casket and sent to James in Scotland. Equally moved, James wrote a poem about his favourite. In 'The Tragedy of the Phoenix', Stewart is portrayed as a beautiful bird destroyed by envy.

Stewart's letters to James following his exile are extraordinarily passionate. In one letter he writes: 'I desire to die rather than to live, fearing that that has been the occasion of your no longer loving me.' Stewart tells the king he wishes 'to dedicate myself entirely to you'; he prays that he may die for James to prove 'the faithfulness which is engraved within my heart, which will last forever'. The emphasis on fidelity and passion are clear: 'Whatever might happen to me, I shall always be your faithful servant … you are alone in this world whom my heart is resolved to serve. And would to God that my breast might be split open so that it might be seen what is engraven therein.'

Stewart's profound influence on James can perhaps finally be judged by the fact that James instructed his own son, later Charles I, to look after and protect the whole Stewart family.

*　　*　　*

James had always had an eye on the English throne, knowing that Elizabeth was increasingly unlikely to marry and have children. When Elizabeth died in 1603, James immediately left Scotland for London where he was crowned at Westminster Abbey and took up residence at the Palace of Whitehall. He returned only once to Scotland, in 1617.

The Palace of Whitehall at around the time James took up residence was described in a letter written by Baron Wildstein, a Moravian then living in London. He was clearly astonished at the opulence of what was then one of the sights of Europe. Whitehall, he explains, is 'a palace that fills one with wonder because of the magnificence of its bedchambers and living rooms which are furnished with the most gorgeous splendour'. Whitehall was also the biggest palace in Europe.

*   *   *

The second of James's great male loves was Robert Carr (1587–1645). James met Carr in 1607 when the young man fell from his horse during a jousting match. Carr was just twenty, while James was forty-one; James was smitten and in the years that followed he made it abundantly clear that Carr was his new favourite – he was first made a Knight of the Garter and a privy councillor, then Viscount Rochester and finally the Earl of Somerset. Carr married Frances Howard after James corruptly engineered her divorce – he appointed bishops to an ecclesiastical court prepared to agree to the divorce solely to please Carr.

James's love for Carr seems eventually to have backfired. Once ennobled, Carr appears to have neglected the king, who was furious. James no doubt felt rather used – he must have realised that having got what he wanted from him, the young favourite was happy to move on. In an extraordinary letter James complains that Carr has been 'withdrawing ... from lying in my chamber, notwithstanding my many hundred times earnest soliciting you to the contrary'.

The courtier Thomas Howard noted how James could barely keep his hands off Carr. James, we are told, 'leaneth on his arm, pinches his cheek, smoothes his ruffled garment'.

Events took a bizarre turn at around this time when Carr's wife was accused of poisoning her husband's best friend Sir Thomas Overbury. In a sensational trial – the judges no doubt leaned on by James who was out to get his revenge – the couple were found guilty and sentenced to death. Unable to see the man he loved executed, James had them imprisoned in the Tower of London. Here they stayed for seven years before James forgave them and banished them to their country estate. By this time, James had also moved on to the man who was to prove the greatest love of his life.

James was in his forties when he fell in love with George Villiers, later the Duke of Buckingham (1592–1628). The two men had first met in 1614 but, with the loss of Carr in 1615, James's need for a new romantic liaison became more intense. The pattern of earlier loves was repeated and by 1623 Villiers had been offered a dukedom. This was an extraordinarily rapid promotion for a man of relatively lowly rank and inevitably it caused comment and jealousy among James's more senior aristocratic courtiers. But as with his earlier loves, James refused to see reason where Villiers was concerned, writing to him in December 1623:

> My only sweet and dear child, Notwithstanding of your desiring me not to write yesterday, yet had I written in the evening if, at my coming out of the park, such a drowsiness had not come upon me as I was forced to set and sleep in my chair half an hour. And yet I cannot content myself without sending you this present, praying God that I may have a joyful and comfortable meeting with you and that we may make at this Christmas a new marriage ever to be kept hereafter; for, God so love me, as I desire only to live in this world for your sake, and that I had rather live banished in any part of the earth with you than live a sorrowful widow's life without you. And so, God bless you, my sweet child and wife, and grant that ye may ever be a comfort to your dear dad and husband.
>
> James R

It is difficult to believe that such a passionate letter could have stemmed from mere brotherly affection; in its details, the letter suggests something far more intimate.

So, who was George Villiers and how did this extraordinary and deeply scandalous relationship with James begin?

Villiers came from a long line of minor Leicestershire gentry. Records show that the Villiers were originally gentleman farmers – they owned rather than rented their land – but George's father, who was also named George, had moved a little further up the social ladder by becoming a high sheriff for Leicestershire and an MP. The family had lived at Brooksby, Leicestershire since at least the mid-thirteenth century. Villiers's mother Mary was ambitious for her son and sent him to France to learn the manners and skills that would lead, she hoped, to a career at court. By today's standards, a career as a courtier was no career at all. It relied on a young man simply making his presence felt one way or another. Almost anyone dressed appropriately could attend the court at Whitehall and if by wit or good looks he could catch the attention of the king, he might quickly find himself allowed to accompany James on his walks around the gardens and courts of the Palace of Whitehall. If he happened to be especially attractive, for whatever reason, the king might insist he be present regularly. Formal preferment might begin in as casual a manner as that. In James's case, good looks were vital if one hoped to be noticed and Villiers had the great good fortune of being exceptionally handsome.

There is no doubt that James's relationships with both Stewart and Villiers were seen at the time as scandalous because they hinted so strongly at physical need. As we will see, James's letters to his favourites have an almost desperate air which may well stem from the lack of affection typical of royal childhoods at this time. The idea that children were fundamentally different from adults – an idea developed only in the nineteenth century – would have seemed bizarre; children, especially royal children, were simply seen as miniature adults who had no need of extra affection. James, as an adult, whatever the truth about his sexual orientation, was desperately in need of affection – and that affection was most readily found in his male favourites. Yet James himself, in his book *Basilikon Doron* ('royal gift'), had written that 'Sodomy is a crime ye are bound in conscience never to forgive.'

Basilikon Doron was written in 1599 and intended as a guide to kingship for James's son. The book may well have included this advice because the king himself knew from his own experience how dangerous homosexuality could be to a king. He also perhaps feared that it might be something he had bequeathed to his son. It is a truism of parenting, even royal parenting, that we try to steer our children away from what we see as our own mistakes.

Certainly, whatever the deeper motives for the advice he gave his son, James could not give up Villiers whatever the risks of continuing the relationship. When his Privy Council protested at his extravagant treatment of his favourite, James wrote:

I, James, am neither a god nor an angel, but a man like any other. Therefore, I act like a man and confess to loving those dear to me more than other men. You may be sure that I love the Earl of Buckingham [Villiers] more than anyone else, and more than you who are here assembled. I wish to speak in my own behalf and not to have it thought to be a defect, for Jesus Christ did the same, and therefore I cannot be blamed. Christ had his John, and I have my George.

To Presbyterian ears James's claim that 'Christ had his John, I have my George' must have seemed close to blasphemy. However, clearly James felt that few would dare suggest his relationship with Villiers was anything more than close friendship. Certainly, at this time, close – sometimes very close – relationships between men were not unusual. We in the West are sometimes surprised today to see in strict Muslim societies such as Saudi Arabia men walking together hand in hand. In such societies this is simply an act of close friendship and something rather similar was possible in early modern England. When James refers to 'sodomy' in *Basilikon Doron*, he means very specifically the act of anal penetration; this was a capital offence at the time, but intimate friendship between men – even to the extent that male friends might sleep together – was perfectly acceptable. Where we today might see being gay as an identity, being gay in early modern England would have been specifically restricted to the act of sodomy. Of course, where a man was overly physically affectionate with another man, rumours might begin to spread. But close male friendships were important; arguably more so than they are today.

Friendship, especially intimate friendship between men, could and often did lead to professional success. Indeed, it was essential to it. As the great Elizabethan courtier William Cecil wrote to his son, 'a man is advanced as he is befriended'.

The problem with James was that he took the relationship with George Villiers beyond the limits of friendship and made it look either as if Villiers had demonic powers over him or that the two men were involved in a forbidden relationship. The evidence for a friendship bordering on obsession is clear. Within a year of the two men's first meeting in 1614, Villiers had been knighted. In 1616 he was made a viscount and a year after that he was offered an earldom. Titles were bestowed at what seemed an almost frenzied pace: in 1618 Villiers became a marquess, in 1619 the Lord High Admiral and, finally, in 1623 he was appointed the Duke of Buckingham and there is no doubt that if there had been an honour higher than duke, Villiers would have been offered it.

Contemporaries were frequently aghast at the two men's public displays of affection. The diarist and MP Sir John Oglander confided that he had never seen 'any fond husband make so much or so great dalliance over his beautiful spouse as I have seen King James over his favourites, especially the Duke of Buckingham'.

Suspicions swirling around James's male friendships dated back to the earliest years of his time in England. Soon after he was crowned King of England and Ireland in 1603, a scurrilous Latin epigram quickly became common currency among the literate classes: 'Rex fuit Elizabeth, nunc est regina Jacobus' ('Elizabeth was king, now James is queen').

But what hard evidence is there for a physical, sexual relationship between James and Villiers? Well, we know that James and George shared a bed – long after the two men had become inseparable, Villiers recalled in a letter to the king the time they had spent together in 1615 at Farnham Castle in Surrey. Villiers wonders 'whether you loved me now ... better than at the time which I shall never forget at Farnham, where the bed's head could not be found between the master and his dog'.

James's harsh condemnation of sodomy in *Basilikon Doron* does not necessarily mean his relationship with Villiers was not physical, since 'sodomy' referred to a very specific act. James no doubt convinced himself that any kind of physical expression of his love for Villiers was acceptable so long as it stopped short of penetrative sex ('sodomy'). Whatever the exact nature of their physical relationship, James took great risks in the manner in which he defended the relationship.

But if there were any doubts that James regularly spent the night with Villiers, whatever that might precisely entail, such doubts were dispelled when recent work at one of James's favourite residences – not a palace but certainly a great house – revealed an extraordinary hidden structure.

James visited Apethorpe Hall in Northamptonshire regularly and spent a great deal of time there with Villiers. Apethorpe was built in the fifteenth century for Henry VIII; it was inherited by Elizabeth I and, following Elizabeth's death, by James. During restoration work in the early twenty-first century, a secret passage was discovered in the house, linking what was known to have once been James's bedroom with rooms occupied by George Villiers. Now perhaps more than ever we know why Apethorpe was one of James's favourite houses.

But still doubts remain for, as we have seen, there were precedents for intense male friendship at this time; friendships that were sometimes held up as an ideal in human relationships. Historian Keith Thomas gives a splendid example in his book *The Ends of Life: Roads to Fulfilment in Early Modern England*. When Sir William Neville and Sir John Clanvowe died outside

Constantinople in 1391, they were buried in a single tomb with their helmets kissing and their coats of arms combined, a practice normally reserved for married couples. They became an example mentioned frequently down the centuries of the epitome of love. But the notion of human friendship as an ideal to which all men should aspire has more ancient origins. The great Roman orator Cicero had said that without a friend, life was not worth living and James would certainly have agreed with him. Friendship between men and women did not fit this category of disinterested love because social norms meant relationships between men and women were defined by marriage and sex – women might be daughters, wives or mistresses, but not friends, or at least not friends with men to whom they were unrelated.

*　　*　　*

As monarchs increasingly became aware of the need to listen to their advisers and indeed to Parliament, they turned inwards and personal relationships took on a greater importance. It was also far easier for a monarch to maintain relationships that for lesser men and women might have led to censure or even the gallows. A forbidden relationship with a young man would endanger a monarch only if that relationship threatened the nobles' power or seemed in any way seriously to undermine them. James took risks but unlike Edward II he was not reckless.

Among his highly educated courtiers James could hide his relationships with men such as Villiers and Stewart behind idealised pairs of same-sex friends of whom most educated people would have been aware. Examples from the Bible and from literature were well known, including Musidorus and Pyrocles from Sir Philip Sidney's famous *The Countess of Pembroke's Arcadia* and Shakespeare's Hamlet and Horatio.

Though he trod carefully, James certainly made mistakes. His obsession with Stewart and later Villiers did occasionally threaten his position – he was unsure how to deal with the English Parliament, for example, and relations deteriorated to such an extent that he suspended Parliament in 1621 having effectively lost that body's confidence. His inability to find an accommodation with his fractious ministers was attributed to his obsession with his favourites.

But things had changed since Edward II was deposed. The monarchy had come to seem less an institution led by an unusually valorous and warlike individual and more like an institution that had an existence independent of a particular monarch. In the Middle Ages, there seemed always to be numerous potential claimants to the throne – and any such claim might be enforced in battle. When William of Normandy invaded Britain to unseat Harold, for example, his claim was based largely on the fact that Edward the Confessor had named him as his successor, but of course there was no hard evidence for this. William was also related to Harold and the English royal family (even though Harold was Danish), but his aim was not to prove his right to the English throne via the law courts but rather via the battlefield. Edward II's nobles took things into their own hands by killing Piers Gaveston, but it is difficult to imagine Villiers being assassinated in a similar way by the aristocrats surrounding James. The chivalric world and all that went with it had largely vanished by the time James came to the throne. That world, so typical of how we think of the medieval period, is described by Keith Thomas in *The Ends of Life* as follows: 'In this … [world] personal glory could be more important than the achievement of the military objective. Commanders were more concerned to make a name for boldness than for judgment and they preferred to fight alongside their troops in the front line rather than to conduct operations from the rear.'

For James, this kind of personal hyper-masculinity was far less important than it had been for Edward so his affairs with young male favourites were less of an issue. We see in James the early signs of a diminishing of the monarch's power as an individual political actor and it is this that leads us eventually to modern constitutional monarchy, where, stripped of real power, kings and queens increasingly used their position not to control events in the wider world but to control individuals near at hand for their own pleasure. As figures encouraged to think of themselves from birth as enormously important yet increasingly sensing their lack of power in the wider world, monarchs inevitably felt their need for action thwarted – except in the area of personal relations.

This reached its apogee in Charles II and, later, in the reign of Edward VII. Charles established a court where morality was laughed at and pleasure was the sole aim of life. Edward VII paid lip service to the puritanical morals of an earlier age, but was a serial adulterer and perjurer.

Of course, James's reputation suffered from the rumours that swirled around him, but James would never have been so foolish as to give his favourites anything beyond titles and money, unlike Edward II who gave Gaveston the powers of a Regent.

The scandals surrounding both Edward II's and James's same-sex relationships have about them an element of what we might now call the 'Houdini complex'. Both kings seemed to enjoy living – and loving – dangerously; getting themselves into scrapes from which they could escape only with difficulty. This was clearly far truer of Edward and Gaveston than of James and his favourites, but it speaks volumes about the curious needs generated in monarchs who, though pampered and fawned over, remain perpetually conscious that their palaces are to some extent prisons; their cages may have been gilded, but they were cages nonetheless.

As we will see in later chapters, modern royals also suffered and suffer the damaging psychological effects of living in gilded cages and more today than ever that manifests itself in the Houdini complex – brought up in supremely privileged yet constrained environments, princes and princesses feel compelled to live dangerously, to misbehave and then frantically to try to escape the consequences of that misbehaviour.

James certainly saw his personal position as unassailable. He was, he insisted, next only to God. Addressing Parliament in 1610 he said: 'The state of monarchy is the supremest thing upon earth; for kings are not only God's lieutenants upon earth, and sit upon God's throne, but even by God himself they are called gods.'

Others have not had such a high opinion of James. The

eighteenth-century English philosopher Jeremy Bentham wrote that James's condemnation of sodomy in *Basilikon Doron* had a false ring to it: 'If he ... reckons this practise among the few offences which no Sovereign ever ought to pardon, this must ... seem rather extraordinary to those who have a notion that a pardon in this case is what he himself, had he been a subject, might have stood in need of.'

Rudyard Kipling, writing in the early twentieth century, was entirely dismissive of James:

> The child of Mary Queen of Scots
> A shifty mother's shiftless son,
> Bred up among intrigues and plots,
> Learned in all things, wise in none.
> Ungainly, babbling, wasteful, weak,
> Shrewd, clever, cowardly, pedantic,
> The sight of steel would blanch his cheek.

But perhaps the last word on this most scandalous king should go to James's contemporary, King Henry IV of France, who said James was 'the wisest fool in Christendom'.

CHAPTER FOUR

CHARLES II AND THE TRICK WORTH FORTY WENCHES

'With my prick I'll govern all the land.'
JOHN WILMOT, EARL OF ROCHESTER

Much of the history of royal morality in the past four centuries can be seen in terms of swings between extremes. The dour Puritan era of mid-seventeenth-century England under Oliver Cromwell was followed by the riotous immorality of the reign of Charles II; the morbidly repressed era of Queen Victoria was followed by the sexual abandon of her son Edward VII. Closer to our time, the rigidly moral George V was followed by his playboy son Edward VIII.

When the Puritans enjoyed their brief period of real political power under Cromwell, there was a sense that somehow almost all pleasures were sinful – in 1647 during the so-called Protectorate, even celebrating Christmas and Easter was banned; the theatres were closed; and dancing involving men and women was prohibited. The Puritans believed the state should enforce their harsh view of Christianity, but inevitably they squabbled among themselves since their absolutist attitudes meant no two Puritan groups could agree on exactly how a good Christian society should be run and no group was prepared to compromise with any other.

After the Restoration of 1660, it was as if the country breathed a sigh of relief. At last life could be about more than churchgoing and prayer. To the horror of Puritan fundamentalists, the population once again revelled in pleasures that had been denied them for a generation. Leading this new charge was Charles II (1630–85), a man who had grown up in France, was almost certainly a Catholic – he was formally to convert to Catholicism on his deathbed – and enjoyed, to the exclusion of almost everything else, the pleasures of the flesh.

It was almost as if Charles saw the radicals who had signed his father's death warrant – Puritans to a man – as representing a lifestyle and an attitude to Christianity he was determined to reject. He paid lip service to the forms of Anglican worship, but devoted himself to a life that was entirely irreligious and scandalous in the extreme. His palaces, especially Whitehall, became lodging houses for prostitutes and his numerous mistresses. Even while his harem lived cheek by jowl in their luxurious apartments, Charles made sure his own apartments were the closest to the river so that young women, procured specially by his servants, could be brought to him quietly and discreetly at night.

To the population of London and indeed farther afield,

Charles's desire for pleasure – and his refusal to condemn those who drank to excess, visited brothels and the theatre and slept with each other's wives – made him immensely popular. In this respect, his effect is remarkably similar to that of Edward VII, whose scandalous life – as we will see – made him popular because it followed half a century of officially sanctioned gloom dominated by his overly censorious, indeed puritanical, mother.

Such was the thirst for fun that even Charles's mistresses became popular figures in their own right. Most famously we remember Nell Gwyn (1650–87), whom Charles first spotted outside the Covent Garden playhouse selling oranges, or so the legend goes. When the London mob decided they hated Louise de Kéroualle, one of Charles's Catholic mistresses, it was not because she was a mistress but because she was Catholic. Nell, by contrast, was always popular. Seeing the king's coach near Charing Cross and with a woman inside, an angry crowd gathered thinking the woman was Louise. They began to shake the carriage and throw stones. Realising she might be in real danger, Nell leaned out of the coach window and shouted, 'Pray good people be civil, I am the Protestant whore.' The crowd lifted their hats to Nell and cheered!

The word 'whore' was a largely descriptive term during the Restoration with less of the sense of absolute moral condemnation it acquired in the nineteenth century. Stories of cheeky Nell Gwyn were common during her lifetime. When Charles visited her in her lodgings near Drury Lane on one occasion, she decided he must do something for her son by him. She waited until the king was seated and seeing her young son playing in the corner of the room shouted: 'Come here you little bastard!' The king was horrified. 'Do not call him that,' he is said to have responded. 'Why not my lord,' said Nell, 'for he hath no other name'. Charles promptly created the young boy Earl of St Albans and from that day on the family enjoyed the privileges of wealth and rank.

Tucked away in apartments and courtyards right across the sprawling Palace of Whitehall, there were at least thirteen official royal mistresses by 1670, not to mention Charles's wife, and he was generous to them all. He usually had at least half a dozen active mistresses at the same time and they frequently made his life a misery by complaining bitterly about each other and continually trying to obtain money and privileges for either themselves or their children by Charles. Nell was the least grasping and Charles, fully alive to her good nature, begged his heir, later King James II, 'Let not poor Nelly starve.' It was almost the last thing he said.

For a monarch such as Charles II, the Palace of Whitehall – with its intricate maze of rooms, apartments, courts, towers, cellars and passageways – was a perfect place to indulge his sexual appetites. As Don Jordan and Michael Walsh point out in *The King's Bed: Ambition and Intimacy in the Court of Charles II*, the palace:

> was home to a vast array of residents: royal relatives, both near and distant, mistresses current and passed-over, court favourites, amusing confidants, tedious advisors, well-fed Beefeaters, bawdy laundresses, gentle seamstresses and household and kitchen

staff of all varieties, along with the King's personal herbalist, his chemist, pimpmaster and pox doctor. All these and more lived cheek by jowl, a whole city crammed into a palace.

All around the garden and dotted here and there throughout the palace were not just Charles's current mistresses, but also his discarded ones – for however much he might have fallen out with them, he never made them homeless. And besides, if he tired of his current favourite, he might always rekindle his interest in an older favourite who was almost always close to hand and ready at a moment's notice to do his bidding. If ever a king exercised his royal power to get what he wanted, that king was Charles II.

The price Charles paid for his scandalous love life was that he inevitably became the target of satire and jokes, which detracted from both his reputation and his effectiveness as king. Unlike his father Charles I and his brother, who was to become James II, Charles II knew that a king must bend to some extent to the will of Parliament and of the people. The will of the people might be difficult to define precisely, but even a king would ignore it at his peril. Charles was astute enough to understand this. Though Catholic in his sympathies, he was careful not to upset the Anglican scheme of things in England. His brother James, by contrast, was far more autocratic by instinct. Despite the risks and upset it caused, when James became king following the death of Charles II, he began to appoint Catholics to every high office. The result inevitably was the so-called Glorious Revolution and James's loss of the throne and exile. Charles, though scandalous in his private life, was careful not to scandalise the established order.

When, for example, Charles issued his Royal Declaration of Indulgence in 1672 – a remarkably modern gesture of tolerance designed to remove many of the restrictions and penal laws directed at Catholics and nonconformists – Parliament quickly forced him to withdraw it and to impose the Test Act instead. This declared belief in transubstantiation, a central tenet of Catholic faith, as 'superstitious and idolatrous'. It also imposed a rule that everyone in public office must agree to receive only the Anglican sacraments. Charles I would have gone to war over this humiliation. Edward II would have simply refused. But Charles II explicitly and implicitly accepted that the will of Parliament must ultimately prevail. He knew that the road to absolutist rule could lead only to the sort of struggle that had ended in his father's execution.

*　　*　　*

Like Edward II and James I, Charles had his favourites but he only rarely allowed them to be seen to be exerting too much political influence on him. It was almost as if he enjoyed stirring up just enough trouble to annoy Parliament and his more serious advisers without provoking them to action. Of course, Charles had the great advantage over his scandalous predecessors in that he did not become besotted with men; Charles's favourites were always women and given the constraints on women at the time – the fact that they could not hold any political office – he was

on safer ground. However much Charles showered his mistresses with money and their children with titles, the nobility would
not feel threatened as they had by Piers Gaveston and George
Villiers.

The curious thing about Charles is that, deprived to a large
extent of political power, he seemed almost to cultivate his
reputation as the merry monarch. It is as if, unable to do as he
pleased in the public sphere, he was determined to do what he
wanted in the private sphere: the sphere of pleasure. And when
it came to pleasure, Charles was notorious. Few monarchs
would have reacted as Charles did to the scores of scurrilous
and often obscene verses written about him, very often by his
friends. Edward II would have reacted with murderous rage to
the sort of public mockery Charles seemed to enjoy. He might
easily have had those who ridiculed him executed or at least
imprisoned. But Charles very rarely acted against those who
portrayed him as a sex-obsessed hedonist.

*　　*　　*

One of Charles's greatest friends at Whitehall was John Wilmot,
Earl of Rochester (1647–80). A man of self-confessed amorality,
Rochester reflects perhaps more than any other individual of the
time the true nature of Charles's court. The king's preoccupa-
tions and enthusiasms were Rochester's and both men shared an
obsession with sex; but it was even more shocking that Rochester's obsession included both women and men.

Rochester was far more intelligent and gifted than Charles

and even while he indulged his every desire there was a part of him that regretted the pointlessness of a life of debauchery. It might even be that he felt a certain disgust at his own indulgences. The same was certainly not true of Charles, who encouraged Rochester to ever wilder excesses. In his verse, Rochester attacked himself at least as much as he attacked the king. He was like a modern rock star hell-bent on self-destruction, but he was also a fine poet who, towards the end of his life, wrote 'To the Postboy', a deeply damning poem about his own life:

> Son of a whore, God damn you, can you tell
> A peerless peer the readiest way to hell?
> I've out-swilled Bacchus, sworn of my own make
> Oaths would fright Furies, and make Pluto quake;
> I've swived more whores more ways than Sodom's walls
> E'er knew, or the College of Rome's Cardinals:
> Witness heroic scars, look here, ne'er go,
> Cerecloths and ulcers from the top to toe;
> Frighted at my own mischiefs I have fled,
> And bravely left my life's defender dead;
> Broke houses to break chastity, and dyed
> That floor with murder which my lust denied:
> Pox on it – why do I speak of these poor things;
> I have blasphemed my God and libelled kings:
> The readiest way to hell – come, quick, ne'er stir.

And then follows the devastating final line, spoken by the postboy: 'The readiest way, my Lord, 's by Rochester.'

Rochester's wit and nihilism, his addiction to drink and women, both reflected and inspired the spirit of the age. He is above all things a guide to the royal scandals of his time; scandals that had their source in the behaviour of the king. Of course, for ordinary people, the working poor, the tradesmen and merchants, the spirit of the age was much as it had always been. Only the upper classes and the aristocracy were swept up in a world where almost anything was acceptable. Rochester's most famous lines on King Charles were written, according to the diarist Thomas Hearne (1678–1735), 'on occasion of his majestie saying he would leave everyone to his liberty in talking when himself was in company, and would not take what was said at all amiss'.

Rochester promptly wrote the following:

> God bless our good and gracious king
> Whose promise none relies on;
> Who never said a foolish thing,
> Nor ever did a wise one.

Rather than stand on his dignity and punish Rochester, Charles, a witty and intelligent man in his own right, responded by saying: 'This is very true: for my words are my own, and my actions are my ministers'.'

One or two of Charles's more serious courtiers – the descendants no doubt of the barons who deplored Edward II's love of rowing, hedging and ditching – wanted Rochester punished for this, but the king would have none of it. Why? The reason is that Charles loved to see how far others would go if they were unconstrained by his presence. Like many monarchs, Charles knew that those who flattered him did so only because he was the king. If he insisted people could speak as they chose, he took a risk but knew he had a better chance of hearing what people really thought. It must have been deeply refreshing – and occasionally infuriating.

Charles also enjoyed being entertained and Rochester – with the quickness of his wit and his outrageousness – was the most entertaining of his companions. In an age of social media and television we forget that without these things conversation and company were of enormous importance, especially for the leisured classes who had long hours to fill and no formal work. Thomas Hearne recalled an occasion when a group including Charles and Rochester were drinking and making jokes about each other. Charles stopped mid-sentence and asked Rochester to create a verse on the spot satirising the king's companions. Rochester replied in an instant:

> Here's Monmouth the witty,
> And Lauderdale the pretty,
> And Frazier, that learned physician;
> But above all the rest,
> Here's the Duke for a jest,
> And the King for a grand politician.

The brilliance of this is lost on us today until we remember that the Duke of Monmouth was notoriously dull and the Duke of

Lauderdale was famously ugly. The reference to a duke who is otherwise unnamed is to James, Duke of York, later James II, who was completely lacking in a sense of humour. The reference to the king is a more subtle and gentle dig. Only Frazier, the king's physician, escapes a drubbing.

But there was a darker side to Rochester and indeed to the age over which Charles presided. Free of the constraints of conventional morality, Rochester drifted into alleged atheism, writing:

> After death nothing is, and nothing, death:
> The utmost limit of a gasp of breath.

And Rochester's lack of restraint meant he could circulate the most extraordinary pornographic verses without any risk of censure from the king and his more conventional advisers. One of Rochester's most popular poems, circulated in many copies during his lifetime, was 'A Ramble in St James's Park'. It seemed to sum up the attitudes and values of what was perhaps the most scandalous period in English royal history:

> Much wine had passed, with grave discourse
> Of who fucks who, and who does worse
> (Such as you usually do hear
> From those that diet at the Bear),
> When I, who still take care to see
> Drunkenness relieved by lechery,
> Went out into St James's Park

To cool my head and fire my heart.
But though St James has th' honor on't,
'Tis consecrate to prick and cunt.

Charles loved such verses precisely because they were so scandalous. Sex was by far the king's favourite pastime and he gloried in the fact that his friend Rochester was able to capture this in his poetry.

Churchmen and those of a more serious turn of mind, including the diarist John Evelyn (1620–1706), were horrified at the immoral behaviour of the upper classes and the court. Evelyn, who was a great supporter of the monarchy, thought Charles would have been a good ruler 'if he had been less addicted to women'.

But there was nothing anyone could do since many of the great aristocrats who surrounded the king were, like Rochester, drunk on the extraordinary freedoms of the age. The Puritans believed that the theatre encouraged licentiousness and they must have been horrified when not only did Charles allow them to reopen but he allowed women to perform for the first time.

What would once have been seen as an immoral life – a life that might lead to criminal prosecution – had become the norm, for where the king led, the aristocracy, to a large extent, followed. That scandal and immorality had seeped deep into the cultural attitudes of the time can be judged by the numerous Restoration plays whose main theme is that of stupid middle-class people, especially those from rural areas, being duped by sophisticated urban types who know there are only two things worth living for: money and sex. Mostly the satire is not aimed at the immoral characters – they are presented as admirably clever, witty and sophisticated; they are individuals we are meant to admire because they are not hidebound by outmoded ideas about morality.

The court's intimate connection with the theatre can be judged by the fact that the king's mistress Barbara Villiers (1640–1709) was so taken by William Wycherley's play *Love in a Wood* that she became Wycherley's mistress. Wycherley (1641–1716) was particularly admired for a later play, *The Country Wife*, which was considered so scandalous even in its own time that it was banned from the stage until 1924.

The play's central character Horner (almost certainly based on Lord Rochester) pretends to be impotent in order to seduce as many wives as possible, including the innocent country wife of the title. But Wycherley was only one of a number of Restoration playwrights who, freed from the constraints of the church and conventional morality, were able to write plays that completely rejected the idea of the 'moral' life in favour of a life of pleasure. This life of pleasure most shockingly included sex with boys. Rochester writes:

> Then give me health, wealth, mirth and wine,
> And, if busy love entrenches,
> There's a sweet, soft page of mine
> Does the trick worth forty wenches.

Charles was prepared to forgive his favourites their lechery, their seduction of each other's wives, their satires and even the seduction by others of his own mistresses, but on at least one occasion Rochester wrote something so offensive that for a time the king banished him from court. 'A Satyr on Charles II' is remarkable because it is an attack on the king that lacks Rochester's trademark humour and its tone is almost savage:

I' th' isle of Britain, long since famous grown
For breeding the best cunts in Christendom,
There reigns, and oh! Long may he reign and thrive,
The easiest King and best-bred man alive.
Him no ambition moves to get renown
Like the French fool [the French king, Louis XIV], that wanders
   up and down
Starving his people, hazarding his crown.
Peace is his aim, his gentleness is such,
And love he loves, for he loves fucking much.

In the scandalous world inhabited by Rochester and other members of the king's circle, this might have caused little more than amusement, but Rochester's poem continues:

Nor are his high desires above his strength:
His sceptre and his prick are of a length;
And she may sway the one, who plays with th' other,
And make him little wiser than his brother [James, Duke of York].

This was beginning to look like a suggestion that the king's mistresses were exercising power through the king – far more dangerous than the mere suggestion that the king was a sex addict. And Charles would have known that this poem was circulating among important people at court.

Rochester continues with a couplet that seems to be an attack on himself and the other courtiers with whom the king spent his time, not for their wise advice but rather because they amused him:

> Poor prince! Thy prick, like thy buffoons at Court,
> Will govern thee because it makes thee sport.

The final couplet caused most offence:

> All monarchs I hate, and the thrones they sit on,
> From the hector of France to the cully of Britain.

This was too much even for Charles and indeed Rochester knew he had overstepped the mark because a letter that has survived indicates that Charles was never in fact meant to see the poem. The anonymous letter dated January 1674 is quoted in K. H. D. Haley's book *William of Orange and the English Opposition, 1672–74*, published in 1953. Whoever wrote the letter, it is clear they were close to the king and aware of how far jokes and satires were allowed to go: 'My Lord Rochester fled from court some time since for delivering (by mistake) into the king's hands a terrible lampoon of his own making against the king, instead of another the king asked him for.'

We know that Rochester tired eventually of his dissolute life, though there is no evidence the king shared the sense of pointlessness expressed in some of Rochester's later poems. Certainly it is doubtful he ever reached the depths of cynicism expressed in the opening lines of Rochester's 'A Satyr Against Reason and Mankind':

> Were I, who to my Cost already am,
> One of those strange, prodigious Creatures *Man*,
> A Spirit free, to chuse for my own Share,
> What Sort of Flesh and Blood I pleas'd to wear,
> I'd be a Dog, a Monkey, or a Bear;
> Or any thing, but that vain Animal,
> Who is so proud of being Rational.

*　　*　　*

Rochester and other courtiers were known to share each other's mistresses and Rochester even gave advice to the king's lovers on how to remain in the king's good books. *The Rochester–Savile Letters, 1671–80*, edited by John Wilson and published in 1941, include this from Rochester to Nell Gwyn: 'Cherish his love wherever it inclines, and be assured you cannot commit greater folly than pretending to be jealous; but on the contrary, with hand, body, head, heart and all the faculties you have, contribute to his pleasure all you can and comply with his desires throughout.'

This sombre advice had its poetic counterpart. In 'A Satyr on Charles II' Rochester writes:

> This you'd believe, had I but time to tell ye,
> The pains it costs to poor, laborious Nelly [Nell Gwyn],
> Whilst she employs hands, fingers, mouth and thighs,
> Ere she can raise the member she enjoys.

* * *

Then we come to the servants. To what extent were they involved in the scandals, the atmosphere of uncontrolled sexuality surrounding the king and his court?

With absolute power to control his private life, Charles was able to indulge every appetite and though much of the atmosphere of the time is brilliantly captured by Lord Rochester, less is known about the practicalities – the means by which Charles procured women and girls and had them brought to him at Whitehall. Evidence is inevitably scant but tantalising scraps suggest that at least one of Charles's servants, William Chiffinch (or Cheffin, the spelling varies), regularly obtained young women for Charles. Chiffinch was one of three generations of the same family who worked for the royal family; the Chiffinchs were trusted implicitly and among their duties was sourcing lovers for the king. To make this easier, Charles's private apartments were next to a landing stage on the Thames. Being very close to the river was considered unhealthy – mists and fogs were thought to spread infection, the air was often damp and the river was polluted – and yet Charles was insistent that his apartment at Whitehall should be immediately next to the river, while his mistresses had apartments much further back, towards modern Whitehall and the Banqueting House. Whenever Charles wanted a new lover – she might retain his interest for one night, several weeks or longer – Chiffinch would secure the services of one of the hundreds of young prostitutes who plied their trade in the Haymarket and outside the theatres. The young woman would be delivered discreetly by river boat to the king and whisked away just as discreetly the next morning. The need for discretion was not based on Charles's embarrassment about these young women; it had a great deal to do with the violent jealousy of his more aristocratic mistresses, especially Louise de Kéroualle.

Sexual intrigue was relatively easy to hide at Whitehall because the palace's interlinking courts and alleyways were largely open to the public and it would have been easy and unexceptional for a senior servant such as Chiffinch to be seen going in and out with anyone he chose day or night. We must not think of Whitehall as anything at all like Buckingham Palace, a single large house with just one or two entrances. The Palace of Whitehall was a honeycomb the size of a small town, and Charles and his Page of the Bedchamber exploited this.

However hard Charles tried to be discreet, the details of his lifestyle were common knowledge. The Puritans, of course, hated him, but not just for his shameless promiscuity. They hated him far more for his supposed Catholicism or at least sympathy towards Catholics. An anonymous versifier, with obvious Puritan sympathies, wrote of Charles:

> A man of words and not of deeds,
> Is like a garden full of weeds.

But whatever the Puritans thought of him, Charles was at least remarkably self-aware. He wrote: 'I have always admired virtue but could never imitate it.' He was also able to laugh at himself. Addressing one critic, he said: 'You had better have one king than one hundred.'

And he was genuinely tolerant of religious difference – he would have agreed with his ancestor Elizabeth I who said we must not 'make windows into men's souls'. Even when criticised directly and without the humour that usually accompanied Lord Rochester's slights, Charles could be remarkably tolerant. The Quaker Robert Barclay took a huge risk when, in November 1675, he wrote directly to Charles:

Thou hast tasted of prosperity and adversity; thou knowest what it is to be banished thy native country, to be overruled as well as to rule and sit upon the throne; and being oppressed, thou hast reason to know how hateful the oppressor is both to God and man. If after all these warnings and advertisements thou dost not turn unto the Lord with all thy heart, but forget him who remembered thee in thy distress and give up thyself to follow lust and vanity, surely great will be thy condemnation.

Had Barclay written to Henry VIII in these terms, he might well have ended his days in the Tower of London. But Charles's reaction to the letter was to ask what he could do to lessen the discrimination against Catholics and dissenters.

Politically, too, Charles was far more astute than some historians have allowed. Having sued for peace over the Dutch War (1672–78), he worried that Catholic France might invade England so he negotiated an agreement – having used his sister as a go-between – that he would announce his decision to become a Catholic if the French King Louis XIV would agree to an alliance. Robert Bucholz and Newton Key, writing in *Early Modern England, 1485–1714*, point out that key to Charles's political and social success was that 'he forgave most of those who had tried to destroy him during the Protectorate'. The poet John Milton was allowed to live, for example, despite having written a justification for the execution of Charles I. Bucholz and Key see Charles's desire to live only for pleasure as a direct result of his experiences in exile:

Basically, Charles II was a cynic – and who could blame him? After all, the people who now professed their undying loyalty and affection for him were the very ones who had fought against his father. He would never fully understand their prejudices. On his last visit to his dominions in 1651 he had been forced to hide in a tree before sneaking out of the country in disguise. During the ensuing exile of over eighteen years, he had been threatened, denounced, promised to, lied to, used, and spied on by them – as well as by every government in Europe. Often, he would find that a confidential servant was in the pay of his enemies; or that a fellow monarch had used him as a pawn in some diplomatic game of chess with Cromwell. No wonder that he trusted no one. He never knew when the English, Scots, and Irish would change their minds once more and force him to go 'on his travels' again.

So, perhaps understandably, the young ... king decided to make hay while the sun shone.

An equally considered but contemporaneous account of Charles's character comes from one of his chief ministers, George Savile, Marquess of Halifax, who wrote:

It must be allowed he [Charles] had a little over-balance on the well-natured side, not vigour enough to be earnest to do a kind thing, much less to do a harsh one; but if a hard thing was done to another man, he did not eat his supper the worse for it ... this Prince might more properly be said to have *gifts* than *virtues*, as affability, easiness of living, inclinations to give, and to forgive: Qualities that flowed from his nature rather than from his virtue.

Certainly, virtue in the modern sense was a word that could never be applied to Charles II, but his life of pleasure must have seemed a reasonable compensation for the loss of political power. It is also important to remember that the king was able to combine almost absolute power over his friends and mistresses, his court of wits, with a life of absolute luxury in his palaces, especially the two almost contiguous palaces of Whitehall and St James's.

The two palaces were separated by St James's Park which, as we saw in Rochester's poem, was itself a centre of pleasure and intrigue; here prostitutes of all classes mingled along with women of the court – all hoping to attract the king's attention during his regular walks in the park. The rewards of becoming the king's mistress outweighed any disadvantages.

For all Charles's focus on pleasure as a guiding principle in life, he allowed his ministers to do their work and accepted their advice, especially, for example, that of Edward Hyde, 1st Earl of Clarendon. On Hyde's advice, Charles issued the Declaration of Breda in 1660, which expressed the king's desire for a widespread pardon for all those involved in the English Civil War. The declaration was also a statement of Charles's acceptance of the importance of 'liberty of conscience, an equitable settlement of land disputes and full payment of arrears to the army'.

This was issued just before Charles returned to England as king in 1660 but it was typical of his reign that he did his best to adopt a policy of live and let live. Many of his contemporaries were astonished, for example, at the number of his former enemies – enemies who had worked assiduously for Cromwell – who were allowed to stay in post after 1660.

Accepting the advice of Hyde and others was probably only partly the result of Charles's continual awareness that he must not fall out with Parliament. His main reason for following Parliament's advice was that his focus was, as we have seen, inwards rather than outwards, private rather than public. His youth had been blighted by insecurity: having narrowly escaped from England with his life after famously hiding in an oak tree, he lived an impoverished and, as he saw it, humiliating life in France. He never forgot this, or indeed recovered from it, and on his return to England was determined simply to make up for lost time.

*   *   *

We must remember, too, that for all his scandalous, even immoral, lifestyle, Charles was one of the greatest royal patrons of the arts. Under Charles, literature and the theatre flourished in England; he was a libertine but he was also a libertarian who believed that to a large extent his subjects' private lives should not be a matter for Parliament or him. In this respect he is a remarkably modern figure.

Charles also temporarily ended, at least for the upper classes, the long tradition of religious obsession with sexual morality. Restoration London was in many ways similar to the swinging 1960s, at least for those with money and position.

Such was Charles II's enormous influence that, a century after the Restoration, London, and especially St James's Park and the surrounding area, still reflected the kind of scandalous sexual freedom that Charles had encouraged. James Boswell, the great biographer of Samuel Johnson, writes in his journal for 25 November 1762:

I went to Love's and drank tea. I had now been some time in town without female sport. I determined to have nothing to do with whores, as my health was of great consequence to me. I went to a girl with whom I had an intrigue at Edinburgh, but my affection cooling, I had left her. I knew she was come up [to London]. I waited on her and tried to obtain my former favours, but in vain. She would by no means listen. I was really unhappy for want of women. I thought it hard to be in such a place without them. I picked up a girl in the Strand; went into a court with intention to enjoy her in armour [an early prophylactic, probably made from sheep's intestine]. But she had none. I toyed with her. She wondered at my size and said if ever I took a girl's maidenhead, I would make her squeak.

The truth is that although Boswell and Charles II and his circle were, if you like, sexually predatory, there was also a belief at this time that women were equally sexually predatory and in a limited way this created an equality that vanished in the nineteenth century. Rochester's poems are full of sexually rapacious women and Boswell describes how enthusiastic his sexual partners were regardless of whether he paid them or not:

I then sallied forth to the piazzas in rich flow of animal spirits and burning with fierce desire. I met two very pretty little girls who asked me to take them with me. 'My dear girls,' said I, 'I am a poor fellow. I can give you no money. But if you choose to have a glass of wine and my company ... I am your man.' They agreed with great good humour ... We were shown into a good room and had a bottle of sherry ... I surveyed my seraglio and found them both good subjects for amorous play. I toyed with them and drank ... and then I solaced my existence with them one after another, according to their seniority.

Similar things happened at Whitehall throughout Charles II's reign, as a long-suppressed play reveals. *Sodom*, which was written in the 1670s and almost certainly by Rochester, can be seen as the ultimate expression of the Restoration court's desire to shock. The play was considered so obscene that copies were not available on the open shelves of some university libraries until the 1970s. Copies were kept – along with copies of the complete Rochester poems – in the *prohibitorum*, a library classification now obsolete. The decision to give this part of a library a Latin name was presumably designed to conceal the nature of the books held from all but the classically educated, who might therefore be presumed (no doubt erroneously) to have only a serious scholarly interest in such books.

The plot of *Sodom* is easily summarised. It begins with Bolloximian, King of Sodom, insisting that homosexuality – specifically sodomy – should be encouraged throughout the kingdom. But the king's chief adviser is sceptical: allowing sodomy will mean soldiers spending less money on prostitutes, and it will leave women, he insists, with no option but to try either dogs or dildos. Other scenes in the play show a prince and princess conducting an incestuous relationship and the queen dying from a sexually transmitted disease. Bolloximian has no intention of giving up sodomy despite the advice of his physician and at the end of the play he insists he will abandon the court for a cave where he can die having sex with his favourite page, Pockinello.

By any standards the language is extraordinary, especially when we remember that the play was probably intended for private performance in front of the king who would have seen aspects of his own character in Bolloximian.

Indeed, Bolloximian's opening speech might be taken as a statement of King Charles's own attitudes and values; perhaps even his whole scandalous reign:

> Thus, in the zenith of my lust I reign,
> I eat to swive [fuck] and swive to eat again.
> Let other monarchs who their sceptres bear,
> To keep their subjects less in love than fear
> Be slaves to crowns; my nation shall be free.
> My pintle shall my only sceptre be,
> My laws shall act more pleasure than command,
> And with my prick I'll govern all the land.

Of course, the play is a satire on Charles's court and it has been said that Bolloximian's promotion of 'sodomy' in the play was analogous to Charles's attitude to Catholicism. But that such a play could be written and circulated at all, and by someone so close to the king, still speaks volumes about the extraordinary sexual and artistic freedoms allowed by Charles II.

* * *

Perhaps the oddest and least known scandal involving Charles concerns his early relationship with Lucy Walter (*c*.1630–58), the woman with whom, perhaps above all others, he was really in love. She was the same age as Charles and they were lovers from around 1648 to 1651 when he was a king in exile; a king without a country and without money. His vast stable of mistresses existed only in the distant future and his love for Lucy was as close to disinterested as an exiled king's could be. She had a son and potentially a daughter by Charles, but, despite his love for her, she seems to have been the only mistress he completely abandoned. In later life he never mentioned her and she eventually moved to Paris where she took a string of lovers simply to pay the bills. Charles had promised her a pension but soon forgot to pay it. It is curious that a king who was never embarrassed to acknowledge his mistresses seemingly forgot about Lucy, but it may well be that Charles had actually married her and he was terrified this would be discovered.

As Lucy was not a Catholic and this was long before the Royal Marriages Act (created by George III in 1772 to stop his children marrying without his permission), the marriage, if it took place, would certainly have been valid and it would make Charles's marriage to Queen Catherine bigamous. No evidence has been found that conclusively proves Charles married Lucy but, until her death at age twenty-eight, she claimed that she kept their marriage certificate in a black box that she had given to the Bishop of Durham, to whom she also confessed that she had married Charles. It seems unlikely that she would have made such a claim – and on her deathbed – given the religious sensibilities of the time and the fear of judgement in the afterlife, but the box, if it ever existed, has never been found.

* * *

Charles II was also involved in a scandal concerning a long-vanished palace of almost unparalleled magnificence. Nonsuch Palace near Cheam in Surrey was built by Henry VIII between 1538 and 1544 at a cost, in 2021 values, of roughly £10 million. It was meant to be the last word in beauty and luxury. The village of Cuddington and its church were razed to the ground to make way for the palace. Hundreds of craftsmen were brought from Italy and they laboured for more than six years along with thousands of workers to create a palace that was the wonder of the world. The very name 'Nonsuch' was a proud boast that nowhere else in the world was there a palace to equal it.

Little more than a century after the palace had been completed, Charles II became fed up with one of his mistresses, Barbara Villiers, Countess of Castlemaine, and her seemingly endless demands for money and attention. He either couldn't or wouldn't give her money so, in 1670, Charles gave her Nonsuch Palace instead. In an act of scandalous vandalism unparalleled before the 1960s, Castlemaine had the enormous palace taken apart and sold brick by brick, marble tile by marble tile, fireplace by fireplace, and all just to pay her huge gambling debts. And so goes what is perhaps the ultimate architectural scandal of the royal palaces.

CHAPTER FIVE

WILLIAM III'S MÉNAGE À TROIS

'Only in our virtues are we original, because virtue is difficult ...
Vices are general, virtues are particular.'
IRIS MURDOCH

Despite a life devoted to sex, Charles II died without a legitimate heir. His brother James (II of England and VII of Scotland, 1633–1701) became king but was famously ousted by a Parliament and a country determined not to have an absolutist Catholic monarch during the so-called Glorious Revolution of 1688. The bloodless coup sent James into exile for the rest of his life and William III (William of Orange, 1650–1702) became king.

William accepted that a condition of his invitation to become king was that he would never seek to exercise the kind of absolutist rule that typified Charles I's reign. Arrogant, ungovernable kings had caused too much trouble in England in the past and had led to the civil war and the execution of Charles I.

But William quickly learned that even a relatively restrained king had no guarantee of popularity. As Sir Robert Walpole (1676–1745) observed, after his coronation in England, William 'met with nothing but disgust'. The English historian John Heneage Jesse (1809–74) explained:

> The appointment of a committee to enquire into the application of his private revenue [he was paid considerably less than his predecessor, James]; the opposition he encountered in obtaining toleration for the dissenting portion of his subjects; the failure of his favourite scheme to introduce … uniformity of worship; and finally, the dismissal of his Dutch guards were sources of severe uneasiness and disappointment.

But William was as determined as Charles II to rule in his private life if he could not rule in his public one so he insisted on living where he chose. 'Soured by his situation,' as Jesse puts it, William left his 'cramped' quarters at St James's Palace for Hampton Court and refused to visit London except on days when Parliament met. He had already decided he hated the Palace of Whitehall because his asthma was made worse by dampness and the fogs of the old riverside residence.

He determined to find somewhere in the country but close enough to London to keep his ministers relatively happy. He chose Kensington, where he bought a small Jacobean mansion from the Earl of Nottingham. William employed Christopher Wren and others to transform what was then known as Nottingham House into the Kensington Palace we know today.

Kensington Palace has been the scene of countless extraordinary scandals, but with the royal family's perfectly understandable determination to avoid washing their dirty linen in public, the details of many of these scandals, both recent and those dating back to William's time, have been revealed in full only over recent decades.

William and Mary (1662–94) moved to Kensington Palace in 1689 and it remained the centre of court life until 1760 when George III decided he much preferred living at Buckingham Palace.

After 1760, Kensington Palace went into a long decline that was only properly arrested in the twentieth century. It slowly became a place where its residents – minor royals and various hangers-on – lived obscure and often eccentric lives. The eccentricities of these minor royals who had little to occupy them occasionally burst into the public consciousness, as we will see.

But Kensington's opening salvo in the scandal wars really began in 1688 when the apparently happily married King William decided to bring to London a young man called Arnold Joost van Keppel (1670–1718). No definitive proof that William and van Keppel were lovers has ever been discovered, but the circumstantial evidence is strong.

Van Keppel was born in Zutphen in what is now the Netherlands. He was a member of a minor aristocratic family, but a family that had become impoverished.

In Bishop Burnet's *History of His Own Time*, published in 1724, there is an intriguing reference to King William behaving in a way that is so scandalous that it cannot be explicitly stated.

Burnet records the Earl of Hardwicke's note that he, Hardwicke, had seen 'a letter of the queen's containing a strong admonition to the king for some gross irregularity of his conduct. The expressions are so general that one can neither make out the fact or the person alluded to. It was thought improper to be published.'

This is odd given that William's queen knew of and accepted that William had at least one mistress. A relationship with a mistress was a fact of court life at the time, especially for a king, and hardly seen as 'irregular'. But a king's intimate, physical relationship with a man was something else.

For centuries, apart from occasional intriguing references such as this, it was always assumed that William had his male favourites but they were just that – favourites. However, there is something about William's excessive devotion to van Keppel that is reminiscent of Edward II's relationship with Piers Gaveston and James I's relationships with his young men.

Whatever else has been said about van Keppel, there is no suggestion that he was in any way effeminate. Part of the reason for his great appeal to William was that he had proved himself in combat. In fact, he was to become the king's closest companion in numerous military campaigns. But given that van Keppel was first brought to London in 1685 when he was just fifteen or sixteen, he can hardly have shown himself so consistently brave in battle by that stage to justify the honours that were quickly heaped upon him.

At just sixteen he was made Viscount Bury; he was already Groom of the Bedchamber and Master of the Robes – both sinecures, highly lucrative posts that involved a large amount of income and almost no work. In 1696 he was created Baron Ashford; a year later he became the Earl of Albemarle, an astonishing elevation for one so young. By 1700 van Keppel had been given vast estates in Ireland, but this was a step too far for Parliament. Ministers insisted the grant of land be rescinded. Furious, William gave van Keppel £50,000 instead and made him a Knight of the Garter.

Rumour at the time swirled around this relationship because as with Edward II and his favourites, William's gifts to van Keppel seemed out of all proportion to what was supposed to be mere friendship. Such favouritism aroused jealousy and deep suspicion; only a man in the throes of a deep, physical passion would throw caution to the winds in such a manner.

It was to some extent William's devotion to the young, handsome van Keppel that led to his enduring unpopularity – an unpopularity that lasted for the rest of his life. Even the news of the king's death in 1702 provoked little mourning, as John Heneage Jesse, writing in 1840, explained:

King William died at Kensington Palace on the 8th of March 1702 ... The funeral ... was conducted in an almost private manner. As an excuse for omitting the customary solemnities, it was affirmed that the expensive war, in which the country was on the point of embarking, would have rendered magnificence alike impolitic and indecent. The true reason seems to have been want ... of affection for him when living and of respect for his memory when dead.

So, what other evidence is there for William's homosexuality? His biographers seem to believe that there is no definitive proof and that anything that suggests he was gay may well have been a deliberate slur by his enemies – and certainly he had detractors. Traditionalists who felt that James was the rightful king never forgave the change of monarch; but William was also unpopular among those who believed that as king, he had right on his side. William's problem was that he was dull and morose; he was neither witty nor charming and he made no effort with anyone except his favourites. His dour treatment of most of his ministers and advisers made a stark contrast with his extravagant generosity to his favourites, so much so that Parliament was alarmed. The real scandal surrounding William was that his behaviour towards his favourites was foolish. Though not as extreme and unthinking as Edward II was with *his* favourites, William nonetheless placed himself in a position where his motives were inevitably suspect. Many even among William's supporters found it impossible to believe that William's relationship with van Keppel was entirely innocent.

Even Gilbert Burnet, the Bishop of Salisbury and sympathetic to William, wrote that William had one flaw which was 'too tender to put into writing'. Given that William had no known vices other than his love for van Keppel, we can reasonably assume that this is what is being referred to.

An anonymous poet of the time summed up the core of the English dislike of William and the fact that already in his lifetime rumours of his homosexual tastes were widely disseminated:

For the case sir, is such,

That the people think much

That your love is Italian

Your government Dutch.

Whatever William said about van Keppel's usefulness as an adviser, we know that his real appeal was the fact that he was young and handsome. The diarist Samuel Pepys (1633–1703), who had no obvious reason to denigrate van Keppel, described him as 'a blockhead'.

And van Keppel was not William's first male favourite. The king had earlier become obsessed with a young aristocrat called Hans William Bentinck, who was born in Diepenheim in the Dutch Republic in 1649 so was more than a decade older than van Keppel.

Bentinck was from an old aristocratic family with ties that criss-crossed Dutch nobility. By his mid-twenties, if not earlier, he had been appointed chamberlain and first page to Prince William. When William became ill with smallpox in 1675, Bentinck seems to have become his chief nurse – even to the extent of sharing the future king's bed during his illness.

On William's recovery, Bentinck, perhaps inevitably after nursing him back to health, became one of his most trusted advisers. So much so that he was a key figure in the complex negotiations to ensure William became king of England. He was the king's chief go-between, raising money and hiring ships and men. Bentinck accompanied William during the invasion of England and was at his side during the 1690 Battle of the Boyne, which finally put paid to James II's hopes of being restored to the throne.

Once William's throne was secure, Bentinck was rewarded with the title of the Earl of Portland. He was also granted more than 130,000 acres in Ireland and would have received additional land in Wales but for the intervention of Parliament. Perhaps this was all just a king repaying his loyal servant, but it was still suspiciously excessive as Parliament's intervention reveals. And Bentinck had long been the focus of rumours – a popular refrain in London was: 'Billy with Benting does play the Italian.' 'Italian' in this context would have been taken at the time to mean homosexual. Indeed, soon after van Keppel's arrival, Bentinck's jealousy of his much younger and prettier rival seems to suggest far more than mere friendship.

Realising he was being supplanted in the king's affections, Bentinck wrote to the king to complain. The letter refers obliquely to rumours that clearly concerned the king's relationship with van Keppel: 'Things I am ashamed to hear, and which I thought you to be as far removed of as any man of the world, [things] I would have thought any man of society would have distanced himself from.'

As with Bishop Burnet, Bentinck cannot quite bring himself to say exactly what is going on. It is all hints and suggestions which have the opposite effect from the one intended – by refusing to state exactly what is going on, Bentinck fuels the rumour mill and makes it far more likely that people will assume the very worst. But perhaps that was always his intention. His letter certainly reads like that of a jealous lover.

The last straw for Bentinck in this ménage à trois came when William insisted on a change in the sleeping arrangements at Kensington. For years William had insisted that Bentinck's apartments should be immediately adjacent to and connected with his own. When van Keppel began to outshine the now ageing Bentinck, the king asserted van Keppel should have Bentinck's residence with its interconnecting doors. Bentinck understandably felt like a rejected lover – rejected just as lovers of powerful men often are in favour of the younger and more beautiful.

Bentinck's hurt can be seen by the fact that he left London and the court permanently in 1699 without telling the king. He also resigned from a string of lucrative offices that had been bestowed on him by William – offices he could have retained if he had simply accepted that van Keppel was the new favourite. But no, Bentinck packed his bags and left Kensington Palace for good.

However, old loves die hard and when William lay dying, Bentinck returned to the palace. The king held his hand and pressed it to his heart as he slipped away.

*   *   *

It has been said that there was nothing suspicious about William's devotion to his favourites; that he was simply a generous man and liked to reward those closest to him. But this is not entirely true. William was in fact notoriously tight-fisted with general expenditure, something that made his wild extravagance to Bentinck and then van Keppel extremely suspicious. William's enemies may have jumped to conclusions about William's elaborate gifts to his favourites, but there is no denying the gifts were excessive. And neither of William's lovers – if indeed they were his lovers – came out of the situation well. Biographer Stephen Baxter, in his 1966 book on William, describes Bentinck as grasping and jealous. Writing well before homosexuality ceased to be a criminal offence, Baxter dismisses the claims that William was sexually attracted to young men by saying he was simply too busy, which seems a remarkably weak argument. But Baxter does neatly sum up the emotionally charged situation as one favourite was supplanted by another:

> For almost thirty years [Bentinck] succeeding in monopolising the interest and friendship of his master; and then the spell had been broken. Keppel was in many ways the image of what Bentinck had been; young, handsome, brave, discreet … Keppel had a number of advantages beyond his exceptional good looks.

Yet those advantages are not really outlined, neither by Baxter nor it seems by any of William's biographers. They all seem to note only the potentially scandalous facts: van Keppel's youth and good looks, the interconnecting bedrooms at Kensington and the extravagant gifts of honours and money.

In his book *Perilous Enlightenment*, G. S. Rousseau sees the relationships between William and his favourites, but especially van Keppel, as symptomatic of a wider scandalous reputation earned by English aristocrats in general. His conclusion gathers together impressions that have their origins, as we have seen, in the outrageous behaviour of earlier kings, most especially James I and Charles II: 'At least since the end of the seventeenth century, when William III and his alleged "catamite" Joost van Keppel ... had crossed over from Holland, the English court gathered a reputation as one of several European centres of aristocratic homosexual licence.'

The truth is that as women were denigrated at this time as intellectually inferior to men, their roles defined as wives, daughters or mistresses, it was very difficult for a king or any man for that matter to enjoy a romantic relationship of equals with someone of the opposite sex. For a man, and perhaps especially a king, it was far easier to invest the need for this kind of relationship in another man. Intense friendships between men were almost encouraged with Biblical and classical ideals providing a kind of background justification. And if such relationships occasionally crossed the line and became physical, that was a private matter of no real importance. The situation is analogous to that which was, and is, common at English public schools – intense friendships between boys often include a sexual element, but the friendship is seen as the key element not the sex. The boys involved do not always consider themselves gay and many cease to have same-sex relationships in adult life.

An unpublished doctoral study by John O'Halloran based on interviews with dozens of young, often aristocratic, men at

English public schools concluded that in the absence of women, the need for intensely romantic relationships found an outlet in relationships with other young men. And if those relationships included sex, it was not usually seen as the defining aspect of the relationship; it was the emotional intensity that was of greatest importance to those involved. This situation may very well parallel the situation in which William and early monarchs found themselves.

*   *   *

Kensington Palace offered William and later monarchs the illusion of privacy; what could not be done at St James's Palace or Whitehall could be done at Kensington. After all, it was a quiet country village until well into the nineteenth century. In William's day, it would have seemed almost remote from the traditional centre of power. But whatever the reason, Kensington Palace seems to have made those who lived there behave in ways they might have thought twice about in other royal palaces.

CHAPTER SIX

DARK DEEDS AT NIGHT: QUEEN ANNE'S LADIES

'Good sooth, she is
The queen of curds and cream.'
SHAKESPEARE, *THE WINTER'S TALE*

There is a curious paradox about the lives of Britain's royal family members: on the one hand, senior royals are allowed almost no real privacy, surrounded as they are by courtiers, servants and advisers; on the other hand, their vast palaces and their power over those closest to them has always created a sense that they can do as they please hidden away behind the high walls of St James's, Buckingham Palace and other great royal residences. Built in what was originally a quiet rural backwater, Kensington Palace seems to have especially encouraged this kind of thing. And the greatest of Kensington's early scandals is that surrounding Queen Anne.

William III died without an heir in 1702, following Queen Mary's death in 1694. Consequently, Mary's sister Anne

87

(1665–1714) became queen. Like William and so many previous monarchs, Anne seems to have quickly fallen under the spell of a number of favourites – much has been written about her relationship with Sarah Churchill, Duchess of Marlborough (1660–1744), for example, and there is compelling evidence to suggest theirs was an intimate, probably sexual, relationship.

As we have seen, showering a favourite with money and honours against the advice of senior figures was always bound to get a monarch into trouble, but things were more complicated with female aristocrats and members of the royal family. Despite the classical education of the male upper classes – an education that would have included texts that referred to Sapphic relationships – few seem to have considered that such a thing was possible in their time. The existence of male sexual relationships was acknowledged as a fact of life, but they were dangerous and could lead to the censure and death even of a monarch, as we have seen with Edward II. But because women were not seen as aggressive actors in relationships or public affairs, and because one woman could not be made pregnant by another woman, sexual relationships between women were seen as either a physiological irrelevance or not truly sexual at all.

Precisely because women were seen as morally and intellectually inferior to men, they were viewed as perpetually childlike; their relationships, even those of a queen, tended to be indulged. Queen Anne could enjoy an intimate, possibly sexual, relationship with Sarah Churchill, and later Abigail Masham (c.1670–1734), that drew criticism, but that criticism was always mild compared with that faced by Edward II or James I, for example.

It is certainly true that having lost seventeen children – all Anne's offspring were either stillborn or died during infancy or childhood – Anne was desperately unhappy. More than anything she needed an intimate physical bond to compensate for the loss of her children. Sarah, Duchess of Marlborough, was in the right place at the right time to provide this. Though she was power and money hungry, there is nothing to suggest that Sarah was entirely cynical in her affection for Anne. Indeed, her friendship with Anne was probably genuine, but she also knew that the more important she became to the queen, the more indispensable she made herself, the more money and titles she would be able to extract from the monarch for herself and her husband. If this meant sleeping with the queen then so be it. Both Sarah and Anne would have grown up with the deeply embedded patriarchal idea that sex is important because it leads to children – to heirs either legitimate or illegitimate. At this time, sex between women was solely about friendship and pleasure and barely counted as sex at all. There were prosecutions of women accused (bizarrely) of 'buggerie', but these were very rare and as historian Margaret Hunt explains, the practice of women sleeping together was so common as not to arouse suspicion:

Girls from poor and middling families generally began working very young ... At some point between about age ten and fifteen many of them were put out to service ... The standard assumption was that they would save their money ... so as to be able to marry some time in their mid- to late twenties. During this lengthy period ... they habitually slept in the same bed with a succession of other girls or women, other female servants if there were any, the daughters of other women of the household, or not uncommonly, the mistress of the house herself ... Many female servants would have experienced the sleeping arrangements of half a dozen households before they turned thirty, and that during a period when they were lonely, often deprived of affection, and, at least part of the time, at a high libidinal pitch. The potential this system offered for risk-free, same-sex erotic activity was very great.

The arrangements in the royal household were not that different and if a queen wanted a favourite female servant to share her bed, suspicion would not have been aroused.

In Queen Anne's case, there is evidence that, for her, sleeping with a female servant would have involved far more than mere companionship. She saw relations with her husband as a dynastic duty, a means to have children; but women were in fact the real focus of her sexual interest. In a letter written in 1708, Sarah Churchill says Anne 'had no inclination for any but [her] own sex'.

Of course, that acknowledged attraction did not necessarily imply a full sexual relationship, as Jyoti Arran Green argues in 'Female Same-Sex Desire in the Nineteenth Century': 'Queen Anne's letters to Sarah Churchill are deeply loving, emotional, and at times erotic, but not explicitly sexual. If, as historians generally suggest, her relationships with women were sexual, it remains vague what exactly is meant by this. Simply sharing a bed? Kissing? Mutual stimulation?'

As lesbian relationships were barely recognised at the beginning of the eighteenth century, they were not formally proscribed. Even if, as seems likely, there was a sexual element in Sarah's relationship with Queen Anne, neither of them – let alone the courtiers who surrounded them – would have considered the relationship a threat to heterosexual norms, which saw sexual relationships as legitimately male–female or illegitimately male–male.

But whatever the exact nature of Sarah's relationship with Anne, it certainly included some form of physical intimacy. Rumours and scandal were able to creep in not because the two women were sleeping together, but because the relationship was seen as corrupting. Anne's behaviour became scandalous because she could not hide the fact that Sarah had too much power over her, and Sarah exercised that power to extract large sums of money from the queen – the court was rife with gossip that Sarah ruled Anne as Anne ruled the country. Knowing that the queen would never complain, Sarah took £12,000 from the privy purse for her own use, followed some time later by £21,000. Even after the two women had fallen out, Sarah helped herself to a final £18,000.

Anne was in an impossible position. If she complained that Sarah was stealing from the privy purse, her courtiers would judge her for having made this corrupt woman the Keeper of the Privy Purse; and given that the queen had also made Sarah the Mistress of the Robes and the Ranger of Windsor Great Park, it might look to the world as if the queen's judgement was seriously flawed.

Early on in the relationship, even her sister Mary had described Anne's passion for Sarah as 'immoderate'. Echoes of this unbridled relationship can be discerned to this day in the wealth and status of the Churchill family – it was Anne after all, in the throes of her passion for Sarah, who pushed for the Churchills to be given the vast estate at Blenheim they enjoy to this day.

It seems very unlikely that Anne would have given the estate to Sarah and her husband John if Anne had not been besotted with her. When the two women eventually fell out, Anne refused even to speak to Sarah and we can imagine how delighted she would have been if only she could have taken Blenheim back.

Of course, written conclusive evidence of a sexual relationship between Anne and Sarah is hard to find. Explicit details would never have been committed to paper by either woman, but the strength of Anne's need for Sarah – her physical need for her – can be judged by a letter she wrote at the height of the relationship. She says:

> Oh, come to me as soon as you can that I may cleave myself to you; I can't go to bed without seeing you … If you knew in what condition you have made me, I am sure you would pity me … I hope I shall get a moment or two to be with my dear … that I may have one embrace, which I long for more than I can express.

Even allowing for the hyperbole that perhaps came more naturally to our ancestors than it does to us, this is pretty strong stuff.

* * *

When Sarah Churchill was supplanted in Anne's affections by her much younger and no doubt prettier relative Abigail Masham, the rumour mill went into overdrive. Despite the protections afforded Anne by her status as a woman and as a queen, the court moved significantly closer to an outright condemnation of a relationship that seemed to have what contemporaries would have described as a scandalous Sapphic element. An anonymous poem that was widely circulated at the time – surely the true measure of how far rumours had penetrated the general consciousness – sums up the general feeling:

> When as Queen Anne of great renown
> Great Britain's scepter sway'd,
> Besides the Church, she dearly lov'd,
> A dirty chambermaid ...
> Her secretary she was not,
> Because she could not write,
> But had the conduct and the care
> Of some dark deeds at night.

* * *

With Anne's death in 1714, the Stuart dynasty finally came to an end but, as we shall see, the Georgians who followed were just as determined to indulge their personal power and desires, however scandalous.

Meanwhile, the rooms at Kensington Palace in which Anne's relationships with Sarah and Abigail were played out remain much today as they were three centuries ago. Partly this is down to luck and the fact that other parts of the palace were repeatedly modernised for new inhabitants until a time came when the early royal apartments seemed too important substantially to alter or destroy. The last serious threat to the palace and its original rooms came in the second half of the nineteenth century, when Kensington came close to complete demolition. It was only Queen Victoria's desire to prevent the destruction of her birthplace that saved the palace. And even that sentiment hid a more practical motive – Victoria needed somewhere to house her numerous relatives and assorted hangers-on.

CHAPTER SEVEN

MONSTERS AND MADMEN: THE HANOVERIANS

'If there is anyone here I have forgotten to insult, I apologise.'
JOHANNES BRAHMS

Among the English royal palaces, Kensington and Buckingham Palace have enjoyed far more than their fair share of scandals. Queen Anne's private life was certainly scandalous, as we have seen, but it was not played out in the public arena. Her intense private life was just that – private.

But Anne was followed by a string of the maddest, most badly behaved monarchs the United Kingdom has ever had to endure. Four Georges reigned from 1714 until well into the nineteenth century; all were undistinguished, widely ridiculed and deeply dysfunctional; one, George III (1738–1820), was actually out of his mind for long periods. Another, the Prince Regent, later George IV (1762–1830), was a byword for unscrupulous greed, selfishness and sexual promiscuity. George I (1660–1727) and George II (1683–1760) were content to live at Kensington while in London; George III and George IV preferred Buckingham Palace.

George I came to the throne in 1714 when he was fifty-four. He had been invited to become king by the English Parliament in the absence of a Protestant heir – neither William and Mary nor Anne had surviving children. George was Queen Anne's second cousin and her closest Protestant relative – more than fifty others had a far stronger claim to the throne, but were rejected on the grounds that they were Catholics.

From the very beginning of his reign, George made clear his dislike of England by spending much of his time in Hanover. England reciprocated by heartily disliking him. On the day of his coronation, there were riots in towns across England. George later spent so much time abroad that a clause in the Act of Settlement (designed to prevent a Catholic ever taking the throne) had to be repealed to allow him to do so. The clause stated that the monarch could not leave the country without Parliament's permission.

The general dislike of George was perhaps best summed up by the great lexicographer Dr Samuel Johnson. Just a few decades after George's death, Johnson wrote: 'George the First knew nothing, and desired to know nothing; did nothing, and desired to do nothing.'

However, if traditionalists felt George had no right to the throne – and there were many who did feel this – few were troubled by his scandalous personal history. But perhaps they should have been for George had an extremely dark past. Before coming to England, like a strange ogre from a children's fairy story, he had arranged to have his wife locked up for life in a remote castle in Germany. And he almost certainly arranged to have her lover murdered.

Long before he had even considered the possibility that he might one day be king of England, George had married, in 1682, a woman who, on the face of it, was never going to be a good match, at least in terms of personality: Sophia Dorothea of Celle (1666–1726) may have been suitably aristocratic, but she was also a high-spirited, fun-loving and extremely sociable woman. George, by contrast, was dour and solitary by nature. His motive for the marriage was money; by marrying Sophia, George significantly increased his income. At this time and until well into the nineteenth century, Germany's large number of tiny principalities meant a large number of impoverished princes. Queen Victoria was later to complain bitterly that her English subjects thought of her princely German relatives as 'paupers'.

Having married George, Sophia gave birth to two children: the future George II in 1683 and a daughter, also Sophia, in 1687. By the time Sophia was born the marriage was already in trouble and George and his wife quickly grew to dislike each other intensely, which is perhaps hardly surprising since the morose, taciturn George was not much of a companion for a woman whose prime aim was to have fun. This incompatibility took a more dangerous turn when Sophia became involved with a Swedish nobleman. It was an accepted fact of life that aristocratic men almost always had mistresses; for aristocratic women, however, the situation was more complicated. If they were discreet and their husbands had lost interest in them, their lovers might be tolerated, but discretion was vital. George would almost certainly have turned a blind eye to his wife's lover, Count Philip Christoph von Königsmarck, but Sophia made the mistake of planning to elope with him.

George and Sophia had long since stopped sharing a bed and George happily consoled himself with his long-term mistress Melusine von der Schulenburg (1667–1743), with whom he had three daughters. However, it was all about keeping up appearances. Despite by now heartily disliking his wife, George was not prepared to be publicly humiliated – as he would have seen it – by her very public defiance of what might best be described as the rules of the game. Once Sophia's possible elopement became known, George and his family acted swiftly. No direct evidence has ever been produced but von Königsmarck vanished, never to be seen again. He was either killed and his body thrown into the river Leine or cut into pieces and buried beneath George's own castle in Hanover.

In some ways George's revenge on his wife was even more savage; she was confined in the remote Castle of Ahlden in Lower Saxony for the rest of her life. Although she had servants, she was forbidden to see her friends or even her children – her servants were effectively her jailers. Her imprisonment was to last more than thirty years, until her death in 1726.

George divorced Sophia in 1694 on the grounds that she had deserted him (which was hardly true) and he made sure that she was stripped of her titles; her name was also removed from all official documents. The divorce judgment against Sophia took no note of the fact that George also had a mistress and imposed

no prison sentence of any kind. George and – rather shockingly – Sophia's own father agreed to Sophia's life sentence. It is
perhaps the supreme example of a monarch using his power to
exert complete control over his personal life.

George may have known nothing as Samuel Johnson put it,
but he was clearly ruthless and determined to do as he pleased.
Like many people who accept a promotion even when they
know they are unsuited to it, George could not resist agreeing to
accept the crown of Great Britain and Ireland even though he
knew he would have much preferred to live quietly in Hanover.
Following the coronation and with more money and status than
he had ever previously enjoyed, George still seemed perpetually
uncomfortable and ill at ease. He never really learned to speak
English fluently and throughout his reign he returned as often
as he decently could to Hanover. In England, he soon realised
that with his ministers making all the real decisions, he could
still have lived a quiet, almost private, life – much as he might
have done in Hanover. Only one thing stopped him – this was
the knowledge that his hated son had set up a rival court to
which the great and the good were being drawn in increasing
numbers. George's problem, as he well knew, was that his court
at Kensington was dull, gloomy and stultifying, whereas the
Prince of Wales's court, at Leicester House in Soho, was a centre
of fun and laughter.

So intense was the mutual hatred between father and son,
which lasted from the boy's young manhood to the end of the
king's life, that the pair were unable to be civil with each other
in public if for no other reason than to lessen the inevitable

damage to their reputations. The Prince of Wales's hatred of his father may well have had a great deal to do with the king's treatment of the young man's mother, locked for ever in her castle in Saxony, but there is no doubt he deliberately tried to create a court that would harm his father by drawing the powerful away from the king. George knew that to counter his son's popularity he would have to give up the quiet life he enjoyed and turn his court into a place of endless fun. Suddenly, from being a palace of dour retirement, Kensington was lit up each week with flaming torches lighting the way across the park to the great gates of the palace. At the balls that became famous, George did his best to seem welcoming and witty, but beneath the surface he was no doubt perpetually fuming at having to constantly endure the limelight simply to try to outshine his own son.

* * *

George's relationship with his son was considered ridiculous, but perhaps no more ridiculous than George himself – the king might have been a good Protestant who had been invited to Britain, but he was still a charmless foreigner who did little to endear himself to his people. His clothes, his accent, his height, his attitudes – all were ridiculed. Even his choice of mistress was seen as absurd. Melusine von der Schulenburg was known as the giraffe or the maypole because she was so thin. George's other female companion, Sophia von Kielmansegg (1675–1725), was famously fat and, perhaps inevitably in the gossipy back-biting spirit of the times, the two women became known as the Elephant and Castle.

George's rage and embarrassment at how he was viewed can easily be imagined, but the situation reached a scandalous peak when rumours began to circulate that the king's relationship with von Kielmansegg was sexual. Having two or three or even a dozen mistresses would not have been particularly frowned upon in a monarch, but von Kielmansegg should have been strictly out of bounds for the simple reason that she was George's half-sister. Historians are undecided about whether the relationship really was sexual, but the difficulty for George was that people chose to believe the rumours. Of course, in living without his wife and with two close female companions, George was breaking the rules – as he was already unpopular, his unconventional life was a gift to his enemies. It seemed that poor George could get nothing right – even his closest advisers, people he might have thought he could rely upon not to believe the rumours about him, were shocked that even if he did not rely on von Kielmansegg for sexual favours, he certainly relied on her for advice. The truth is that George was bored by politics, especially British politics, and he needed his half-sister to help him make sense of it – for whatever else was said about von Kielmansegg, it was agreed that her intellectual abilities far exceeded those of the king. But this was itself considered scandalous. Women were supposed to be inferior to men, especially kings, and yet here was a king who seemed to be able to make a decision only after consulting a woman.

George I was conscious that he had no real power in England and knowing that the British public disliked him, he kept very much to himself. Beyond his mistress and his half-sister, he seems to have had no interests or enthusiasms of any kind. Although, he did hunt at Hampton Court. When Parliament was sitting, he lived quietly at Kensington with his family, until forced to pretend to a sociability he in reality hated. And always beneath this family rift was the dark history of his treatment of his wife – a history that has tarnished his reputation to this day.

* * *

From his first arrival in England, George seemed uncomfortable. He lived for three years at St James's Palace, built on the site of a leper hospice by Henry VIII, but found the small medieval rooms cramped and dispiriting. The great rambling Palace of Whitehall had burned down decades earlier and Hampton Court was too far from the seat of power at Westminster for anything but occasional summer visits. The solution so far as George was concerned was Kensington Palace, and in those first few years in England, George had Kensington remodelled and comprehensively redecorated. Indeed, as he supervised work at Kensington, George showed a level of interest and enthusiasm that was almost entirely lacking for the rest of his reign.

But even here there were difficulties – both the court and the population at large were outraged by George's insistence on surrounding himself with German servants and advisers and much of the work, and expense, involved in enlarging Kensington

Palace became necessary only because these advisers had to be housed somewhere.

George's enthusiasm for Kensington did not last long and he never seems to have lost his longing for Hanover, returning there as often as he could. Indeed, it was en route to Hanover in 1727 that he died, probably from a stroke.

*   *   *

Back in England, the Prince of Wales – now, of course, George II – no doubt rejoiced at the news of his father's death. They had not spoken for years and their relationship had been so bad that the Prince of Wales had been forbidden for years from seeing his children more than once a week – that at least came to an end with George I's death. George II made a good start by dispensing with the services of most of his father's German advisers. And with his more outgoing, sociable manner, he no doubt assumed he was bound to be more popular than his father. In fact, he was heartily disliked. The question is why?

The nineteenth-century novelist William Makepeace Thackeray probably summed up the general feeling about this second George when he wrote: 'Here was one who had neither dignity, learning, morals, nor wit – who tainted a great society by a bad example; who in youth, manhood, old age, was gross, low, and sensual.'

Dysfunctional families often hand misery and unhappiness on from one generation to the next and the Hanoverians were no exception. Logic would say that a man hated by his father might make every attempt to ensure that his children escaped such intergenerational animosity. This seems to have been beyond the Georges. George II was hated by George I and George II's son and heir Frederick (1707–51) became the focus of an intense, almost pathological, loathing. What made this even worse was that the king's feelings for his son were shared by Frederick's mother, Queen Caroline (1683–1737).

A key factor in this bizarre situation was that from 1714, when he was seven, until 1728, Frederick lived in Hanover while his parents were in England. These were the crucial years when father and son might have developed a reasonable relationship; instead, Frederick arrived in England in no mood to take orders from a father he could hardly remember. George expected his son to defer to him in everything and was outraged when he realised that Frederick had every intention of doing exactly as he pleased without reference to anyone.

But George was in a difficult position. If he completely alienated his son, he knew that Frederick would deliberately set up an alternative court just as he, George II, had done to pique his own hated father, George I. So Frederick was occasionally invited to the court at Kensington Palace, but he was there very much on sufferance – courtiers delighted in discussing the elaborate rituals father and son went through to avoid either speaking to or even looking at each other.

George also persuaded Parliament to reduce the Prince of Wales's annual allowance from £100,000 to just £25,000 in a deliberate attempt to ensure that Frederick was unable to set up any kind of rival establishment. Frederick threatened to petition

Parliament directly for an increase in his allowance – he knew
this would make his father's behaviour a public scandal. The row
reached such a pitch of vindictiveness that George threatened to
evict Frederick and his wife Augusta (1719–72) from St James's
Palace and Prime Minister Robert Walpole had to intervene, as
Lord Hervey recalled in his memoirs:

> Sir Robert Walpole dissuaded them from taking this step; said it
> would put their son more out of their power, increase his party,
> give him the éclat of a separate Court; furnish many people with
> arguments to inveigh against their rigour and keep up the spirit
> of this dispute in the world, if not in their family, much longer
> than otherwise it would subsist; that the suffering their son to
> remain in the palace would have an air of lenity in the eyes of
> some, of contempt in the opinion of others; and that the push-
> ing things to extremity after they had already carried their point,
> would put them in the situation which hitherto their Majesties'
> friends had represented the Prince, and perhaps make the Parlia-
> ment itself less willing to support them when they were oppress-
> ing their son.

So, Frederick and Augusta remained at St James's Palace where,
in order to give the impression of some semblance of normality,
the king and queen occasionally dined with them, but there were
always others present and according to Hervey's memoirs neither
the king nor queen ever acknowledged their son or exchanged a
word either with him or with their daughter-in-law. Indeed, according to Hervey, George and Caroline behaved as if Frederick

and Augusta were invisible. Early on, the bisexual Hervey had been a great supporter of Frederick – they may well have been lovers – but they fell out and became implacable enemies.

Having been forced to be lenient by the Prime Minister, Caroline and George's loathing for their son became almost pathological – Caroline, Frederick's own mother, called him a 'hardened liar', an 'ass' and a 'beast', according to the memoirs of her confidante Hervey.

Few felt that the peace negotiated by Walpole could possibly last and they were right.

The problem was that both sides were always ready to take offence on the slightest provocation. Perhaps the most spectacular incident of this kind occurred when Augusta went into labour in 1736 while the couple were staying with the king and queen at Hampton Court. Instead of letting his father and mother know what was happening – as protocol demanded – Frederick pushed Augusta into a carriage in the early hours of the morning and set off post-haste for London so that the baby would be born at their apartment in St James's Palace. Later that same morning, the king and queen discovered what Frederick and Augusta had done and followed in hot pursuit, convinced the young couple were planning some trickery associated with the birth – the queen had let it be known that she thought her son incapable of fathering a child so she assumed that Augusta's pregnancy was probably fake and that Frederick was planning to introduce someone else's healthy male child as his heir, a so-called warming-pan child slipped into the maternal bed while officials were not looking.

By the time the king and queen had reached St James's, Augusta had given birth to a daughter. Caroline was relieved and no longer suspicious as the couple would hardly have taken the trouble to deceive the monarch over a mere daughter – and the child died a few months later anyway. The queen's attitude to her son did not soften.

For George, Frederick's deliberate attempt to keep him away from the birth was the final straw. Apparently unembarrassed at how childish and spiteful it would appear to those around him, George wrote to family members and all his ministers warning them that any contact with his son would mean permanent banishment from the king's presence.

Punishment for Frederick and Augusta was immediate: having been evicted from Kensington Palace, they were now also evicted from St James's Palace and forced to rent a house from the Duke of Norfolk in St James's Square.

As time passed an uneasy stalemate developed but privately the king and queen became increasingly obsessed with the idea of preventing their son from ever becoming king. They were advised that nothing could be done constitutionally, so it is easy to imagine their joy when Frederick died suddenly aged just forty-four in 1751, leaving the way clear for Frederick's son to become George III on the death of his grandfather. Caroline did not live to see the long-hoped-for death of her son – she had died in 1737 – but would no doubt have been just as delighted as the king, her husband.

The feud between George II and his son – a feud played out so scandalously and so publicly – was an extraordinary repeat of George II's own relationship with his father, George I. In its extravagance it also perhaps says a great deal about the underlying mental instability of the Hanoverians and their descendants. Incredibly, some element of the antagonism between one generation of royals and the next was to continue after the death of George II with varying degrees of unpleasantness, through every reign until that of Elizabeth II.

*　　*　　*

The Hanoverian kings were deeply unpopular in England; their only virtue in many people's eyes was the fact that they were not Catholic. George I and II were mocked for their German accents and for their taciturn, charmless personalities. They were ridiculed, too, for their apparent half-hearted interest in England. George II, for example, spent many summers back in Hanover and he made no secret of his preference for living in Germany. While he was away he left his wife Caroline as Regent, a decision that initially seemed eccentric given that strictly speaking he should have left his son Frederick in his place. The difficulty was that he hated Frederick. If people expected Caroline to be hopeless they were greatly mistaken, for Caroline was highly intelligent and knew far more about politics than her errant husband.

Though it may seem perfectly sensible to us to leave an intelligent woman in charge, this was viewed at the time as yet another example of the outrageous behaviour of the Hanoverians. It was bad enough to hate your son and heir, but to allow a woman to run the country really was unforgivable. And yet even her contemporaries acknowledged that Caroline would have made a far better monarch than her dull-witted husband. She took the business of government very seriously, enjoyed political discussions and no doubt revelled in her chance to show how astute she was. Whenever George was away, she insisted on regular meetings with her Privy Council and held public days at Kensington Palace on Sundays when anyone who looked and sounded right might be admitted – hundreds usually turned up and jostled for places in the state rooms.

Where George seemed always to be ill at ease, Caroline, by contrast, was very much in command. She was also astute, announcing that she would rather live on a dunghill than return to Hanover, a statement that immediately endeared her to her adopted country. Her friend John Hervey wrote of her: 'The darling pleasure of her soul was power.' Her interest in the individuals who exercised that power, and in the machinery of government, explains why her ministers so valued her judgement.

However, in contrast to her sure touch as Regent, Caroline, like her husband, was a disastrous parent. Her first-born son, Frederick, whom she hated, was certainly a difficult character, but he was not the black-hearted villain she imagined him to be. Her third son, William Augustus, Duke of Cumberland, by contrast, was seen by both Caroline and George as a model son.

William Augustus became known as 'Butcher Cumberland' following his victory at the Battle of Culloden in 1746. The English had little sympathy with the Jacobite rebels, who, as we will remember, aimed to overthrow the Hanoverians and replace them with Charles Edward Stuart, the Young Pretender, the grandson of James II, the ousted Catholic king. But Cumberland's savagery, his attempt to wipe out the Highlanders and their wives and families, made him deeply unpopular. For the rest of his life he remained baffled that his actions in Scotland had made him such a hated figure in England.

By the time George III came to the throne in 1760, following the death of his grandfather George II, the Hanoverians seemed far less alien than they had seemed even a generation earlier. And a major change was in store, for no sooner had he been crowned, than George moved from Kensington Palace to Buckingham Palace, which has been the monarch's favourite palace ever since. Kensington was no doubt far too closely associated with family nightmares!

*   *   *

Looking back from the perspective of the twenty-first century, it is impossible to view the Hanoverians as anything other than both mad and bad. As we have seen, both George I and George II hated their eldest sons to an almost insane degree and in George III dysfunction and eccentricity finally became real madness. For much of the twentieth century, medical historians argued that George III's 'madness' was caused by porphyria, a disease of the liver that results in intermittent confusion and seizures, but more recently it has been argued that George was actually suffering from bipolar disorder.

Whatever the exact nature of his mental difficulties, George

III was very different from the previous Georges. Unusually, he was devoted to his wife, Queen Charlotte, and had no interest in taking a mistress – a significant break with tradition. However, the king's fondness for his wife did not mean he was going to take a more tolerant attitude to his numerous offspring than his predecessors; in fact, George III was just as determined to control his children as any of his forebears.

His obsession with the need to control his own family became so intense that he insisted his ministers draw up what became known as the Royal Marriages Act of 1772, which forbade members of the royal family from marrying unless they had first obtained the monarch's permission. This Act, which might easily have been repealed by a future monarch, was to lead to deep unhappiness in succeeding centuries, most notably in the case of Queen Elizabeth II's sister Princess Margaret who was unable to marry Group Captain Peter Townsend without her sister's permission.

But if George III was a famously devoted family man, he was more famously a man prone to bouts of insanity. It was as if family dysfunction had crystallised at last into genuine madness. And George's bouts of insanity grew worse as he grew older so that for the last years of his life, he had to allow his eldest son, later George IV, to rule as Regent. And of all the royal males Britain has produced, the Prince Regent must count as the most scandalous.

During his periods of madness, George III was kept at Kew Palace (at that time still deep in rural Surrey), so that his strange behaviour could be concealed, so far as possible, from the public.

George's periods of insanity had one major benefit. Right up until the time of the king's first mental collapse, all mental illness had been treated in an astonishingly brutal manner. In what seems to us a remarkably primitive attitude even for the eighteenth century, it was assumed by doctors that the mentally ill were inhabited by demons and if those demons could be beaten out of the patient all would be well. This led to appalling cruelties, but the doctors treating George III could not bring themselves to inflict similar cruelties on him. Gentler means were tried to help him and this resulted in a revolution in the treatment of mental illness from which we still benefit today.

The greatest disaster that resulted from George III's mental problems was arguably the simple fact that because he was often unable to perform the duties of the monarch, his son, the Prince of Wales, took charge as Regent.

The story of the Prince Regent is almost legendary. Suffice to say that he was a man who lived what might well be seen as the ultimate life of self-indulgence. Where George III had avoided scandal in his private life, George Augustus Frederick, his eldest son, seemed to relish scandal. Though the Prince Regent was a significant patron of the arts – he commissioned Jeffry Wyatville to remodel Windsor Castle and backed John Nash's spectacular plans for the development of Regent's Park and Regent Street, as well as Nash's work on Buckingham Palace and the Royal Pavilion, better known as the Brighton Pavilion – he was also extraordinarily addicted to lying, cheating, collecting mistresses and eating and drinking. He lost millions on foolish bets – he once bet on which of two raindrops would first reach the bottom of a window at his club and on another occasion lost a huge sum after betting on the number of cats he would see while walking up Bond Street.

Indeed, so reckless was the Prince Regent that it was felt by some that he shared his father's propensity to insanity. Though not officially mad in the sense his father was, he was certainly unbalanced. The sense that, as heir to the throne, he could more or less do and say as he pleased never left him. He was an alcoholic who became grossly obese yet insisted to anyone who would listen that he was also an active military man – on one occasion while dining with the Duke of Wellington, the hero of the Battle of Waterloo, the Regent told the duke how, during that battle, he had charged down a particularly steep slope at the head of his men. The duke drily responded: 'Yes, very steep, sir.' As Wellington knew well, the prince had been in England during the Battle of Waterloo.

The poet and politician Winthrop Mackworth Praed, who knew the Prince Regent, summed up what many thought of him:

> A noble nasty course he ran
> Superbly filthy and fastidious
> He was the world's first gentleman
> And made that appellation hideous.

The Prince Regent's conviction that he was a heroic soldier was matched by his obsession with his own magnificence. And wherever he lived he felt it was necessary that his surroundings should reflect his own view of himself. Thus, he spent millions transforming Carlton House in St James's into a magnificent palace in the 1780s, only to have it demolished when he came to the throne in 1820 because it was too small for a king. By the mid-1790s his debts amounted to more than £650,000 (equivalent to £70 million in 2021). Most of this had been spent on entertaining, building, rebuilding, gambling and women. George III agreed to pay these debts only if the prince agreed to marry his cousin, Princess Caroline of Brunswick (1768–1821). Seeing no other way out of his financial situation, the Prince Regent agreed. But he was so horrified when he saw his bride for the first time, that he staggered, gasped and asked for a large glass of brandy. He continued to drink throughout his wedding day and was so drunk by the time he and Caroline went to bed that night that he slept on the floor at the foot of the bed.

The prince and Caroline seemed intensely to dislike each other almost from the word go, yet they managed to produce one child, Princess Charlotte born in 1796, who was to predecease her father. It was the Prince Regent's outrageous treatment of his wife that fixed for ever his reputation as a scandalous monarch; a monarch who caused serious damage to the whole idea of monarchy in the United Kingdom.

After Caroline and George parted company for good in 1796, Caroline went to live at Kensington Palace where she gained a reputation for eccentricity. She saw her visitors in the morning while still in her nightclothes – a deeply shocking breach of etiquette – and began to dress in an increasingly bizarre fashion, occasionally wearing strange hats including one made out of a pumpkin.

But if Caroline was unconventional and sometimes shocking, she was also perceived as harmless. She kept a low profile and left England in 1814. Like her husband, she had a number of affairs. The prince and Caroline might have muddled along like this indefinitely, but when George III died in 1820 and the Prince Regent ascended the throne as George IV, he decided it was time to divorce Caroline. But here a difficulty arose. He was told that if he sought a divorce on the grounds of Caroline's adultery, she would almost certainly counter with details of his far more numerous adulterous relationships, which were widely known. To get round the problem, the king asked his ministers to draw up what was eventually called the Pains and Penalties Bill, the sole purpose of which was to divorce Caroline without going through the courts and risking public exposure. The new king was no doubt deeply shocked at how unpopular this Bill quickly became – so much so, in fact, that it had to be withdrawn.

Furious, George insisted that Caroline should never be referred to again by his ministers or ambassadors from foreign states. He even instructed the clergy not to include mention of her in their weekly prayers. Caroline countered by insisting she would attend her husband's coronation in July 1821.

In one of the most bizarre public royal spats in history, Caroline reached Westminster Abbey and was turned away at the door, but she was cheered by the public; when the obese, drug-addled George arrived, he was greeted with boos and hisses. The scandal of king and queen at loggerheads might have continued indefinitely, but for a curious coincidence – a coincidence that has led to rumours Caroline may have been poisoned. Foul play has never been proved but George must have been delighted when he heard that Caroline had fallen ill on the day of the coronation. She died just a few weeks later on 7 August 1821, insisting on her deathbed that she had been poisoned.

George's hatred for Caroline was so intense that he even punished the places in which she had lived. For example, after having been forced to allow Caroline to live at Kensington Palace, he made sure no repairs were ever carried out. When she left England in 1814, he stripped her apartment bare – the furniture and pictures, even the fireplaces were sold off. Even more vindictively, George insisted that the house she had lived in at Blackheath be razed to the ground. He wanted the demolition carried out in such a way that no trace of the house should remain. It was thought he had been successful but in the 1980s a tiny part of the house was rediscovered. If you want to see where Caroline once bathed at Montagu House you still can – the sunken bath with its short flight of steps is still there in today's Greenwich Park.

* * *

Throwing himself into an insane life of pleasure was George's reaction to an over-controlling father and a cold, unfeeling mother, as BBC historian Dr Steven Parissien neatly explains:

The whole royal edifice of sexual respectability and family values which George III had worked so hard to create in the 1760s and

70s was rapidly demolished by his son and heir, brick by brick. And, significantly, as he grew older George's marked preference was not for younger, libidinous lovers but for older, motherly mistresses who were able to offer a degree of sympathy and understanding which he had never received from his own, coldly calculating mother, Queen Charlotte.

In this respect George IV's life almost exactly parallels Edward VII's life and his profound reaction to an equally cold, controlling mother: Queen Victoria. Both men became obese, womanising gluttons, prepared to lie and cheat to get what they wanted.

Like Queen Victoria, George III expected his children to follow his sober, highly moral example, but few of them – certainly not his sons – did so. Both the Prince Regent and his brother Prince Augustus Frederick, Duke of Sussex, married Catholics – the marriages were declared illegal, but in the eyes of many, George IV was still a bigamist. All the sons of George III who survived to adulthood behaved so badly they became known to Queen Victoria as 'the wicked uncles'.

*   *   *

If we search diligently through contemporaneous records it is difficult if not impossible to find anyone prepared to say something good about George IV. His first biographer, Robert Huish, writing in 1830, concluded that 'with a personal income exceeding the national revenue of a third-rate power, there appeared to be no limit to his desires, nor any restraint to his profusion'. According to Huish, George was more guilty of the 'demoralisation of society than any prince recorded in the pages of history'.

Charles Greville, clerk to the Privy Council and a man who knew the Prince Regent only too well, kept detailed diaries through much of this period. Indeed, his diaries are one of the most valuable insights into the Regency. He wrote of George: 'A more contemptible, cowardly, selfish, unfeeling dog does not exist ... There have been good and wise kings but not many of them ... and this I believe to be one of the worst.'

Just a few weeks after George's funeral in 1830, *The Times* put it equally bluntly:

> There never was an individual less regretted by his fellow crea-tures than the deceased King ... an inveterate voluptuary ... of all known beings the most selfish. At an age when generous feelings are usually predominant, we find him absorbed by an all-engrossing selfishness; not merely careless of the feelings of others, but indulging in wanton cruelty.

Perhaps George is best seen as an extreme example of a king who, aware he has no real political power, turns his unquestioned status as monarch into a kind of supreme selfishness. What had once been political power becomes the self-indulgent power to treat other people as playthings – playthings of value only in-sofar as they meet one's own needs and desires. But whichever way you look at it, George IV is the supreme example of a royal behaving badly.

CHAPTER EIGHT

BAD BEHAVIOUR: THE SONS OF GEORGE III

'George the Third,
Ought never to have occurred.
One can only wonder,
At so grotesque a blunder.'
EDMUND CLERIHEW BENTLEY

Hated by his father and his people, George IV proves we don't invariably love merry monarchs who are just too, well, merry. Charles II overindulged in wine and women but he did not seem personally gross. Edward VII came very close to imitating George in his appalling behaviour, his greed and obesity, but then Edward had the advantage of becoming king immediately after the grim, puritanical Victoria, after whom any amount of scandalous behaviour might have looked like a positive outcome.

George IV was the most outrageous of George III's sons, but his brothers were also prone to overindulgence in drugs, alcohol, sex and money and it was their scandalous conduct that pushed Queen Victoria in the opposite direction. She referred to her uncles as 'wicked' and feared them and their bad behaviour. And so, for her, the strict, strait-laced Albert represented a return to the values espoused by George III, values that completely rejected the life of pleasure her wicked uncles stood for.

We know a great deal about the scandalous behaviour of the Prince Regent but much less is known about his brothers. In fact, George III's other sons were almost as bad as their brother, the heir. There is little doubt that their bad behaviour was limited only by their lower status and the fact that they had less money. Parliament might have felt forced to grant ever increasing sums of money to the heir, but it was far less willing to grant money to his profligate younger brothers.

But even constraints on income did little to stop some very odd behaviour in a royal brood that really should have known better.

George III and Queen Charlotte had a total of fifteen children, including nine sons. The brothers who lived into adulthood neatly illustrate a difficulty that remains with us to this day: to what extent should a government allow junior members of the royal family to live at taxpayers' expense? Can the medieval idea be sustained that all princes of the royal blood should be allowed to live in luxury? The idea that only working members of the royal family should be funded by government would have seemed dangerously revolutionary to many in the early nineteenth century, but with so many of George III's sons behaving recklessly, the issue of funding was increasingly debated in public. It was as if having first curbed the political power of the monarchy, government was beginning to see that it might be necessary to curb the self-indulgent private lives of the monarch's family.

In a sense this was an inevitable continuation of the struggle for control between Parliament and the monarch. Only instead of a struggle over who has ultimate power in the political sphere, it became a struggle over who has power in the personal sphere where that personal sphere involves vast amounts of public money. And this is a battle that has yet to be resolved: we are only too familiar in the twenty-first century with the sons of Queen Elizabeth II behaving scandalously while being funded by the public purse.

* * *

George III's second son was Frederick, Duke of York and Albany (1763–1827). Honoré Gabriel Riqueti, Count of Mirabeau (1749–91), said of him: 'The Duke of York ... [is a] mighty drinker, [a] tireless laugher, without grace ... without politeness.' But during Frederick's travels as a young man across Europe, the deference shown to him made him believe he was far more important than he really was. The duke could not see that flattery about his character and abilities was just that – flattery. When he was recalled to England by his father, rather than the self-disciplined, serious and sober character his father had hoped to create, he found a young man whose first act was to set off for Brighton where George III's disgraceful first born, the

Prince of Wales, lived in splendour in the Royal Pavilion, which survives to this day.

The Prince of Wales's habits soon rubbed off on his younger brother. In London, scandalous stories spread quickly and very publicly that the Duke of York was to be found gambling and drinking almost every night of the week at Brooks's Club. Worse, when drunk – and he was rumoured to be continually drunk – he poured scorn on his family and especially his father to anyone who would listen.

Towards the end of the 1780s, the king suffered a particularly serious and lengthy bout of madness. His predicament aroused the public's sympathy, but in the midst of the crisis the Duke of York, with no inkling that he was behaving badly, rose from his seat in the House of Lords and insisted he and the Prince of Wales were being given insufficient money. The duke expressed no sympathy for his father's plight and the public – or at least that part of the public which read the papers and was deemed to be important – was outraged.

Soon after the king recovered, he heard that his second son had fought a duel on Wimbledon Common with a certain Colonel Lennox. If that wasn't bad enough, he'd fought to defend the Prince of Wales's honour after the latter had apparently been insulted by Lennox. The king was furious and determined to remove his second son from the influence of his first.

The king tried what money would do.

Despite already receiving significant funding from the public purse, Frederick was massively in debt from gambling and visiting brothels. The king gave him a house in Whitehall and advised him to go abroad for a while to avoid his creditors. In Germany, Frederick dutifully married Princess Frederica (1767– 1820), a marriage that had been agreed with his father. He returned to England and was promptly awarded an increase in his allowance. The king was convinced marriage would put a stop to Frederick's embarrassing excesses.

In fact, Frederick agreed to the marriage only because he needed the extra money he knew his father would press his ministers to award him if the marriage went ahead. Within months of marrying, Frederick took his money and began to spend increasing periods absent from his wife before leaving her for good three years later.

The duke was unfaithful to his wife almost from the beginning. There were no children and a public scandal was avoided largely because Frederica never complained and lived quietly throughout the thirty years of her marriage to the duke at Oatlands, a large house near Weybridge in Surrey.

The duke might have got away with this but when France declared war on England in 1793, the king insisted that his son take command of the British army, despite his lack of experience.

Like so many royal men then and now, Frederick had been destined from an early age for a military career. At the age of seventeen, he was sent to Germany, still the defining ancestral home of the Hanoverians. He stayed in Germany from 1781 until 1787, studying at the University of Göttingen. In what today looks very much like corruption, the duke was rapidly promoted in the British army during his absence. He became a colonel in the Life Guards in the spring of 1782, major general that same autumn and finally lieutenant general in 1784. All the while he was in Germany. He pursued his military career largely because it had been chosen for him but his real interests – and in this respect he was like most of his brothers – were drinking, gambling (especially gambling) and women.

Historians have long argued about Frederick's merits as a soldier. He did a great deal to streamline the army's organisation, but as an active soldier his career was chequered to say the least. He fought in France, winning battles at, for example, Beaumont in 1794 but also losing – most notably at the Battle of Tourcoing in the same year. The duke's campaigns in France in 1798–99 – by which time he had been promoted to field marshal by his father – damaged his reputation and he was widely mocked, most famously in the rhyme:

> The grand old Duke of York
> He had ten thousand men
> He marched them up to the top of the hill
> And he marched them down again
> And when they were up, they were up
> And when they were down, they were down
> And when they were only half way up
> They were neither up nor down.

Frederick had attempted to annex part of the Netherlands, but after a few minor victories, winter came on and it quickly became apparent that 40,000 British and Russian troops could not simply be kept for months in readiness so a deal was struck with the French to allow the British army to withdraw in return for the release of 8,000 prisoners of war. This severely damaged the duke's reputation. Another popular rhyme hinted at cowardice:

> Calm and serene beyond the cannon's reach
> He shoots the screaming seagull on the beach.

Henry Bunbury had been the duke's aide-de-camp throughout the campaign and fifty years later he published his memoirs under the title *A Narrative of the Campaign in North Holland*. He writes damningly of the Duke of York:

> Much as I loved the Duke personally ... I cannot but acknowledge that he was not qualified to be even the ostensible head of a great army on arduous service ... With a very fair understanding, he had little quickness of apprehension, still less of sagacity ... To these defects must be added habits of indulgence, and a looseness of talking about individuals after dinner which made him enemies.

But if there was scandal surrounding the duke's hopelessness as a general, there was even greater scandal surrounding his choice of mistress.

With his wife safely – and compliantly – stashed away near Weybridge, the duke moved into a house in London's Gloucester Place just off Portman Square with a certain Mrs Clarke (1776–1852). Married to a stonemason as a teenager, Mrs Clarke was inevitably looked down on by the establishment as a common woman who had somehow entrapped the duke. Certainly, he was infatuated with her and her hold on him was widely attributed to her wantonness – that is, her sexual abilities.

It is a truism of history across the world that women are frequently blamed for the misdeeds of men, and this was very much the case with Mrs Clarke. Contemporaries admitted that she was beautiful and extremely vivacious and witty. She had been mistress to a number of increasingly wealthy and powerful men before meeting the duke, who showered her with money that he did not have. In addition to the house in Gloucester Place where she had ten servants and two carriages, the duke bought her a house close to his wife's residence at Weybridge so that he could easily go between the one and the other, when it suited him.

The extent of his passion can be judged from a letter he wrote to Mrs Clarke early on in their relationship: 'How can I sufficiently express to my darling love my thanks for her dear, dear letter! Oh, my angel, do me justice, and be convinced that there never was a woman adored as you are!'

But it was not to last and Mrs Clarke was eventually dropped in favour of a Mrs Cary who lived in Fulham.

Mrs Clarke, in turn, moved on and was offering her services to two of the Duke of York's greatest enemies; one was Major Dodd, the other was almost certainly a man Frederick hated almost more than anyone: his younger brother, the Duke of Kent.

We cannot be certain the Duke of Kent and Mrs Clarke were

lovers, but they were certainly close and Mrs Clarke, no doubt upset at being dropped by her former royal lover, was happy to tell him everything she could that was damaging to Frederick. Mrs Clarke confessed that although she had been treated badly by York at the end of their relationship, he had been generous to her earlier on and indeed generous to her friends in the army. It transpired that Mrs Clarke had been selling army commissions with the connivance of the Duke of York. Eager to disclose anything that would damage his brother, the Duke of Kent arranged for a friend to raise the matter in Parliament.

There was no conclusive proof that Mrs Clarke had sold commissions with the duke's encouragement, but she had certainly sold them. The question a parliamentary commission wanted to answer was: did the duke at least know what was going on?

Mrs Clarke actually had a list of what should be paid to her in return for her arranging various promotions: for a lieutenancy, for example, on full pay, the price was £400; for an ensign, £200.

In voting to censure the duke, Parliament split along party political lines. The opposition always voted against the duke; the government always voted for him. But in the end both sides felt that even if the duke had not known what was going on, he should have. They also knew that a woman with no visible means of support seemed to enjoy the benefits of an enormous income. Mrs Clarke was rather like a modern Russian oligarch who has no legal income yet lives in the most expensive part of London and spends money everywhere at an astonishing rate.

The vote of censure did not pass but around 200 members of the house, a minority, but a substantial one, voted against the duke and he felt he had no option but to resign his military offices. The duke's sisters who had always adored him felt he had been badly abused. Bizarrely, his sister Princess Augusta wrote to a friend blaming all the trouble on 'the Methodists'.

But however culpable the duke, it is difficult not to admire Mrs Clarke's method of exacting her revenge for being dumped. She allowed the newspapers to publish some of the duke's love letters to her with all their baby talk and grovelling endearments. Children in the street no longer shouted heads or tails when they tossed pennies in the air. They shouted 'duke or darling' instead.

But perhaps the highlight of the duke's scandalous life came when, sometime later, the canny Mrs Clarke decided she needed a very large sum of money from her erstwhile lover.

It still rankled with Mrs Clarke that the duke had never given her the pension she felt she deserved, together with a house in a fashionable part of London.

The duke absolutely refused to do anything for Mrs Clarke, but she was a resourceful woman and determined to force him to take action. Legal redress was closed to her – the courts would never take the side of a mistress against a member of the royal family – so she devised a plan to cause him so much embarrassment that he would have to act. Mrs Clarke let it be known that she had written her memoirs and that her book would include a highly detailed account of her affair with the duke. A publisher was delighted to take on the work – there was an enormous appetite at this time for books about the aristocracy so he planned a large print run.

Word of this quickly reached the duke's ears and he knew he was beaten. The prospect of intimate details of his life with Mrs Clarke being made public was too much for him. He bought her a house, agreed to a pension and the book was destroyed.

After a decent interval, the Duke of York was appointed commander-in-chief of the army but, of course, like all such royal military appointments, this had everything to do with his status and nothing to do with his skills.

By 1820 Frederick's debts were so enormous they rivalled those of his brother, the Prince Regent. No one would give him credit. He sold his house at Weybridge but the money had to go to his creditors; he resorted to sponging off his friends and those who wanted to boast they had entertained a prince.

Convinced he would one day be king (his brother, now George IV, having no heir), the Duke of York along with his latest mistress, the Duchess of Rutland, drew up plans in the early 1820s to build a new palace close to the old St James's Palace. As he was now second in line to the throne, he was able to trade on his future prospects (as king he would be in command of considerable patronage) and raise significant sums to buy the land and build his new palace. Yet for reasons that have never been fully explained, but that probably had to do with his notorious unreliability, the promises of funding began to dry up. Before he was able to start work, he was abandoned by those who had given him financial encouragement and the government had to step in to stop his creditors building ordinary houses next to St James's Palace in an attempt to get their money back. Another scandal was averted at great expense and the upside today is that

Lancaster House, formerly Stafford House, was completed by others and survives to this day. It may not have officially been a palace, but when Queen Victoria visited many years later, she said to her host, 'I come from my house [meaning Buckingham Palace] to your palace'.

By the time Stafford House was complete, however, Frederick had died in 1827 from 'dropsy'. He was discovered, 'cold and stiff', sitting bolt upright in his armchair.

And the final indignity came when a monument to the duke was proposed. The Duke of York's column just off the Mall could not find a financial backer: the king, his brother, wanted it built but wouldn't pay for it; none of Frederick's wealthy friends would pay so the government decided to dock one day's pay from every soldier in the British army to finance a monument to a man for whom the population had neither respect nor affection.

So, some of the poorest people in Britain were forced to pay for a monument to one of the richest and most profligate. But from the moment it was completed, the monument became the butt of jokes: it was said that Frederick's column had to be as high as it is – 124 feet – so Londoners wouldn't have to put up with the stink of the duke; others said the column had to be exceptionally high to protect Frederick from his creditors.

*   *   *

But what of George III's other sons, the other wicked uncles?

After the Duke of York came William (1765–1837), later William IV.

William joined the navy when he was just thirteen and saw service in the West Indies and Nova Scotia. In 1781 he sailed to New York – indeed, he is the last British monarch to have visited New York while it was still in British hands.

But like many young royal males, William was not much of a military man. He no doubt thought he was a sailor of genius, but his real qualities were perhaps best summed up in the private diaries of Sir Thomas Byam Martin, one of the officers on board William's ship, the *Pegasus*. According to Byam Martin, the prince 'was deficient in almost all the qualities necessary for a person in high command ... It was therefore better he should be on shore than at sea.'

Disliking his superior officers while on duty in Antigua, the prince sailed without permission for Halifax, an act of gross disobedience that would have led a lesser mortal to be flogged or even executed. Angry at being reprimanded, William committed an even greater offence by setting sail for England, again without permission.

William was back in England by 1789 and furious that he had not been made a duke and given the allowance that traditionally went with that title. He announced that if nothing was done, he would stand as the parliamentary candidate for the House of Commons for Totnes in Devon. Horrified, his father immediately appointed him Duke of Clarence.

He moved to Petersham Lodge, which still stands in Richmond, to the west of London. Just a few hundred yards from the River Thames, Petersham Lodge was built in the early eighteenth century as a grace-and-favour residence, one of a number of properties lived in rent-free and often for life by the monarch's friends and family. Ironically, Petersham was sold by the crown in 1784 only to be bought back by William in 1790. Even today the appeal of the house is clear and especially to a prince who wished to live comfortably and discreetly yet close to London. The house lies behind a high wall and it had been updated in the latest fashion in the early 1780s by the great architect and designer John Soane (1753–1837).

So it was in this house that William set up home with his latest mistress, the delightfully named Polly Finch. Unfortunately, Miss Finch did not last long. During a visit to the Richmond Theatre, William set eyes on one of the greatest actresses of the age – Mrs Jordan (1761–1816) – and was smitten. The duke was twenty-five, Mrs Jordan thirty. She had several children already, fathered by various men. But her acting ability was such that no one would have dreamed of criticising her. For William, she became a substitute mother as well as a mistress. Her maternal qualities were legendary. The essayist William Hazlitt watched her on stage many times. She was, he said, a 'child of nature, whose voice was a cordial to the heart ... to hear whose laugh was to drink nectar ... Mrs Jordan was all exuberance and grace.'

Having resisted the duke's entreaties for several months and realising that none of the fathers of her children were ever going to marry her, she threw in her lot with William and moved to Petersham Lodge. For the next twenty and more years, the duke and Mrs Jordan were inseparable. They spent their time at Richmond or St James's Palace, which Mrs Jordan redesigned and redecorated extravagantly – in his memoirs Charles Greville mentions how uncannily Mrs Jordan's interiors resembled a stage set.

Mrs Jordan bore William at least ten children and their relationship was celebrated rather acidly in verse:

> As Jordan's high and mighty squire
> Her playhouse profits deigns to skim
> Some folks audaciously enquire:
> If he keeps her or she keeps him

After his misbehaviour in the navy, William's requests for a posting in the war against France in the 1790s fell on deaf ears and he spent his time attending the theatre, eating, drinking and seeing his friends, but always grumbling and bitter that his military expertise was not acknowledged.

Then in 1811, William, like his brothers, realised that he could get money from the government if he married and tried to produce an heir. Legend has it that Mrs Jordan collapsed on stage in Cheltenham when she received the news that the duke had decided never to see her again. Like his brothers, William had run up enormous debts despite his huge income – more than £20,000 a year (several million in 2021) – but he wanted more and he knew that marriage would bring him an annual income of at least £40,000.

He paid the abandoned Mrs Jordan an allowance, but critics pointed out it was the least he could do as she was one of the best-paid actors in the country and the duke had lived for years at her expense.

William was nonetheless pilloried by the press for his treatment of Mrs Jordan – who was to die, impoverished, in France in 1816 – but he was too focused now on marriage to mind. He threw proposals at many women – from the heiress Miss Tylney-Long (who would have certainly been rejected by George III) to the Tsar of Russia's sister (who rejected him on the grounds that she considered him an imbecile).

Nothing came of his matrimonial efforts until 1818, when Parliament voted to pay him even more than they had already suggested if he would only marry. The extra money – around £6,000 on top of the already offered £40,000 – was considered derisory by the duke but it was better than nothing and with his father's permission he married the dour evangelical Princess Adelaide of Saxe-Meiningen (1792–1849). Five children were to follow but each died in infancy. Despite his long history of philandering, William appears to have remained faithful to Adelaide.

The duke set up house at Bushey near Hampton Court Palace and was largely forgotten until the death of his elder brother the Duke of York in 1827. Suddenly, William found he was highly likely to become king. Having assumed his naval career was over, he was flattered to be offered the largely meaningless title Lord High Admiral. But old habits die hard and, given nominal command of a part of the fleet, he promptly sailed off without telling anyone where he was going and without permission. His resignation quickly followed. Then in 1830 his brother King George IV died and the duke found himself the oldest British monarch to ascend the throne – aged sixty-four – and with no heir, although there were ten surviving children from his liaison with Mrs Jordan. Like his father George III, William moved to Buckingham Palace but spent a great deal of time at Windsor.

William's short reign – just seven years – was marked by an increasing obsession with his sister-in-law, the Duchess of Kent (1786–1861), and her daughter, Victoria (1819–1901), later Queen Victoria.

William was aware that the Duchess of Kent and her daughter avoided him. Despite the egotism and self-indulgent arrogance that characterised all of George III's sons, William was no fool. Early on he sensed that the Duchess of Kent had her eyes fixed on the possibility of power – he rightly guessed that the duchess hoped that he would die before Victoria reached the age of majority, and that she would therefore be able to govern as Regent. Even more worrying was the fact that it was generally believed that, with the duchess as Regent, the real power would lie with her adviser, the Irish aristocrat Sir John Conroy, a man who ruled the duchess as she ruled Victoria.

William was determined to thwart both the duchess and her adviser, but there was a personal element to these political manoeuvrings – William knew that the duchess despised his brothers and him for what she saw as their deeply immoral lives. She knew the whole history of the brothers' strings of mistresses and illegitimate offspring and her attitude to Victoria's wicked uncles was not the relatively indulgent attitude of the eighteenth century but rather the more censorious, even puritanical, attitude that was to typify England under Victoria.

Personal animosity resulted in the Duchess of Kent making every effort to keep Victoria as far away from her uncle William as possible. But turning down William's regular invitations for Victoria to come to court could be taken only so far.

Eventually, an invitation to dine at Windsor arrived that could not be avoided. Victoria was seventeen and the dinner – a grand and lavish affair – was to celebrate Queen Adelaide's birthday.

The dinner allowed William to make a direct, scathing and very public attack on the duchess. In a speech listened to in stunned silence, he complained that she had helped herself to parts of Kensington Palace without permission and that his one remaining aim in life was to live another year to thwart the ambition of the 'incompetent' duchess and her 'evil advisers'. Warming to his theme, he told the assembled guests that the duchess had 'continually and grossly' insulted him. It is not difficult to imagine the effect this must have had on the duchess sitting just a few feet away.

To the fury of the Duchess of Kent and John Conroy, William, as it turned out, lived just long enough to ensure that Victoria became queen. He died on 20 June 1837; Victoria had reached the age of eighteen just weeks before on 24 May.

*　*　*

George III's fourth son, Queen Victoria's father Edward, Duke of Kent (1767–1820), was yet another failed royal military man. He was ruthless and sadistic – today, he would probably have been found guilty of murder.

Edward was sent to Germany aged eighteen in 1785 to train as a soldier. In 1790 he disgraced himself by going absent without leave. His punishment was a demotion and a posting to Gibraltar. To escape Gibraltar's heat, Edward requested a transfer to Quebec in 1791, believing that the British crown should be, as author Nathan Tidridge puts it, a 'unifying superstructure' in North America. He returned to England in 1800 and in 1802 was made Governor of Gibraltar, but reports began to filter back to England that the duke had been excessive in his disciplining of his men – they were regularly executed for relatively minor infringements.

Indeed, so harsh was his regime of discipline that, fearing a mutiny, the authorities in England recalled him. He was never allowed to return to Gibraltar. The narrowly avoided mutiny in Gibraltar came about as a result of the duke's order that the soldiers were not to drink – at all. But this was just the last in a series of bad decisions. General Barnett, the duke's second in command at Gibraltar, was delighted at the mutiny: 'It is the best thing that could have happened. Now we shall get rid of him.'

Bizarrely and despite his military career having ended almost in disgrace, Edward was appointed field marshal, but it was widely known that the title was, from a practical point of view, meaningless.

The duke had several mistresses, but most famously he spent almost twenty-eight years living with Thérèse Montgenêt (1760–1830), better known by her married name Madame de Saint-Laurent. Rumours suggest they had children but no hard evidence has been found. The relationship ended when, tempted by Parliament's offer of a large increase in his allowance if he married, the duke became engaged to Princess Victoria of Saxe-Coburg-Saalfeld (1786–1861), the mother of the future Queen Victoria.

That summary of the duke's career conceals far more than it reveals. Historian Roger Fulford neatly sums up the general view of the Duke of Kent in his book *The Wicked Uncles: The Father of Queen Victoria and His Brothers*. He was, says Fulford, a 'violent, sadistic lunatic' who would happily have a soldier flogged to death for appearing on parade with a dirty button. For example, on his last day as commander of British forces in Nova Scotia in 1800, the duke left instructions that eleven soldiers were to be executed mostly for trivial offences that no other commander would have seen as warranting such a punishment.

As an adult the duke's daughter Queen Victoria, ever eager to ignore unpleasant realities, always insisted her father was a noble soldier. In fact, like his brother the Duke of York, he was little more than useless as a practical military man. Like all his brothers, Edward complained continually about lack of money and by the time Parliament granted him £12,000 a year in 1799, he had run up debts of more than £20,000.

Back in London and with his military career over, the duke told everyone who would listen that he had been treated abominably. Roger Fulford sums up a problem that afflicted all the sons of George III – one might also say that it is a neat summary of a problem that has afflicted the majority of the sons of the monarch ever since – 'When disaster overtook him, he could not imagine that it might be himself who was to blame.'

Eager to find an outlet for the military power he had lost, Edward determined to exercise absolute control – regardless of expense – over his servants and the houses and palaces in which he lived. He bought a mansion with forty acres at Ealing – hardly a palace, but certainly a place where the duke lived in palatial style with dozens of servants, footmen and gardeners.

Roger Fulford writes:

The happiest time for the Duke ... was at Castle Hill Lodge, a pleasant, low house surrounded by forty acres of parkland. There was a winding drive up to the house which the Duke kept brilliantly lighted at night, every night throughout the year ... There were always six footmen standing at the front door when anyone called ... In the sitting rooms there were bell ropes all along the walls, each of which summoned a particular servant ... The house was filled with musical devices, cages of artificial singing birds, organs with dancing horses, and musical clocks. At night the corridors – all the corridors – and halls were lighted with hundreds of coloured lights.

The duke dismissed criticisms of his spendthrift ways and huge debts. When criticised for running up these debts, he insisted that 'the nation, on the contrary, is greatly my debtor', although of course he did not say why.

From as early as 1798 Edward had also had the use of a large apartment at Kensington Palace. Until his split with Madame de Saint-Laurent, he had fumed at the king's refusal to allow his mistress to live also at Kensington – ever censorious, George III hated the idea that a scandalous relationship should be permitted under a royal roof.

Despite his £12,000-a-year income – more than £1 million in 2021 – the Duke of Kent refused to pay for the refurbishment of the Kensington apartment. The Treasury eventually agreed to fund the repairs, but Edward was never satisfied. For almost two decades, vast sums were spent on the latest wallpapers, an elaborate system of hot water pipes (an early form of central heating), carpets, desks and chairs for the duke's two libraries and a massive reordering of his rooms so his servants would be less obvious when they were moving about. A new grand staircase was also built to provide a sufficiently imposing entrance to the drawing room and dining room.

When he left for Germany in 1818, the duke was still complaining his Kensington apartment was not good enough. When he returned a year later with his pregnant wife, Edward was still obsessed with the need for alterations. He continued to protest about the apartment – and, even more vociferously, about his annual grant – right up to his death in 1820. He died in Sidmouth, Devon after catching a chill which turned to pneumonia. He'd been forced to leave London to avoid his creditors – few of the tradesmen who had worked at Kensington or at his other house in Ealing had been paid and they were now refusing to supply even basic necessities such as food.

A few months before the duke's death, his only child, Victoria, had been born in those perpetually unfinished rooms at Kensington and it was at Kensington, Buckingham Palace and

Balmoral Castle that Victoria was later to plunge into her own scandals.

*   *   *

The fifth of George III's sons was Ernest Augustus, Duke of Cumberland and later King of Hanover (1771–1851). He was compelled like so many of his brothers to join the army and was also a dedicated womaniser. He lived to be eighty, remained rake-thin throughout his long life and was deeply, almost pathologically, unpleasant. His rooms at Kensington Palace were covered in mirrors which might suggest a narcissistic obsession with his appearance. His arrogant, sneering air was so widely noticed that it was said that he was as unpopular in England as Napoleon. His sense of his own importance certainly equalled that of his brothers and he, too, felt he could do no wrong. Like his brother the Duke of Kent, Cumberland also had a sadistic side. He appeared to enjoy inflicting a particularly nasty form of punishment on his soldiers known as 'picqueting' – the practice of forcing a soldier to balance for hours on end on the sharpened point of a stake. His fellow officers could just about tolerate treating the men in this fashion but when he raised his cane to a fellow officer threatening to strike him across the face, his career came to an end.

Stories of his scandalous behaviour were legion – on a visit to a nunnery he is said to have ogled the novitiates and even tried to kiss the abbess. But the greatest scandal surrounding the duke involved the death of his valet.

Lying in bed one night at St James's Palace, the duke was attacked, or so he later claimed, in his sleep. He felt blows to the head, but managed to cry out in time for one of his servants to rush in from an adjacent room. Another servant who also lived in an adjacent room could not be found and when entry was forced to the servant's room it was discovered he had cut his own throat. A jury found the man had committed suicide after attacking the duke, his master. The duke, though badly injured, recovered but his reputation never did. It was widely believed that he had murdered his servant after the man had objected to the duke sleeping with his wife. Cumberland had got away with it, so the rumour went, because he was the king's son.

Even the king despaired of Cumberland. George openly lamented that his son was good for nothing except causing trouble between people. The Prince Regent also hated Cumberland and the feeling, it seems, was mutual. Carlton House, the Regent's magnificent palace at the bottom of Regent Street, resounded to the shouts and screams of the two brothers who could not be together for more than five minutes without violently arguing.

Carlton House faced up what is now lower Regent Street. A house had existed here since the late seventeenth century, but after it was bought by Frederick, Prince of Wales, in 1732 a process of enlargement began which turned a rambling mansion into a magnificent palace. By 1783 Frederick's grandson George had taken possession and it was George who commissioned the fashionable architect Henry Holland to remodel the house. However, by 1785 work on Carlton House became a financial scandal – George was ordered to stop construction after Parliament realised he was commissioning work for which there was no money, largely because George had built up debts amounting to £250,000. Under strict conditions grant was made by Parliament to complete the work but George could never resist buying whatever took his fancy, regardless of whether he had enough money to pay. The extent of his extravagance can perhaps best be judged by the fact that he employed Marie Antoinette's designer Dominique Daguerre to buy furniture for his house. Despite the vast sums spent to create Carlton House, by 1820 George felt that it was simply not good enough and the vast house, a palace in all but name, was demolished. George decided he would much prefer to rebuild Buckingham Palace.

In 1815 Cumberland married his first cousin, Frederica, the Princess of Solms-Braunfels (1778–1841), only to discover that his mother would not meet her on the grounds that she was sexually promiscuous. The details of her sexual adventures were never explicitly stated, but in the row that followed, Queen Charlotte threatened to publish what she knew. She never did, but her son had to accept that his wife would never be welcome at court.

The news that the duke had married scandalously soon spread through the court and out into wider London society. Before long, the following anonymous verse was merrily doing the rounds:

> Of Mecklenburg's illustrious house,
> Soon blessed his arms a willing spouse,
> A tender dame of thirty-four,
> Two husbands she had wed before.

Queen Charlotte never did meet Cumberland's bride, even though she was Frederica's aunt as well as her mother-in-law. After Charlotte's death, her daughters maintained the same attitude. Furious, the duke moved abroad in 1818 and stayed away for sixteen years.

Much of the scandal surrounding the duke stemmed from the fact that he was a violent reactionary who hated anything remotely like progress – it was rumoured that he was so worried that his niece Victoria might become queen and be sympathetic to the Whigs (he was an ardent Tory) that he might even murder her.

When Catholic emancipation became unavoidable in 1829, the Duke of Wellington, terrified at what Cumberland might do, wrote to him telling him not to return to England. A narrow-minded, sinister bigot, Cumberland was nonetheless a man of energy and determination. The diarist Charles Greville recalled: 'There never was such a man, or behaviour so atrocious as his – a mixture of narrow-mindedness, selfishness, truckling, blustering, and duplicity, with no object but self, his own ease, and the gratification of his own fancies and prejudices.'

So loathed was the duke that it was widely believed he had fathered a child – a certain Tommy Garth (1800–73) – with his own sister, Princess Sophia. Garth's father, also Tommy, was chief equerry to George III and certainly met and knew Sophia. He spent the winter of 1799 at Windsor while Sophia was also there. The rumour, which has never been confirmed, spread largely because the princesses were always cooped up by their paranoid parents and desperate for male company, as Charles

Greville explained: 'They [the princesses] were secluded from the world ... their passions boiling over and ready to fall into the hands of the first man whom circumstances enabled to get at them.'

But scandal had still not finished with the duke. As the rumour about his sexual liaison with his sister started to die down it began to be said that during a party in 1829 he had sexually assaulted Lady Lyndhurst, the wife of lawyer and politician John Lyndhurst. The duke insisted to general disbelief that something completely opposite had happened – that in fact Lady Lyndhurst had made disgraceful sexual advances to him. The duke's character had been so blackened that he only had to be seen near a woman for the newspapers to report that immoral or scandalous behaviour had occurred. This reached its lowest point when rumours began to spread that the duke had been having an affair with Lady Graves, an affair which so upset her husband that he killed himself. Lord Graves was comptroller of the duke's household and Lord of the Bedchamber. When the so-called affair took place in 1830, Lady Graves was in her fifties and had fifteen children. But the rumours were enough – Graves wrote to his wife assuring her he believed she was innocent but that same evening he cut his own throat.

The duke was so unpopular that everything bad that could be said about a person was said about him. When his brother William IV died in 1837, the bizarre nature of feudal inheritance came to the rescue of the British public. As a woman, Victoria could not become King of Hanover. Had she been a man, she would have become King of Britain and Ireland and King of

Hanover, but the Salic laws governing the crown of Hanover stated that a woman simply could not inherit the title. So, when Victoria ascended the British throne, Cumberland took her place on the throne of Hanover and the British were rid of him for good. The duke left England with the Duke of Wellington's advice no doubt ringing in his ears: 'Go before you are pelted out.'

The petty squabbles of these most embarrassing royals came to a head when Cumberland returned to England again in 1843 for the marriage of his niece, Princess Augusta. When the time came for the marriage register to be signed, Queen Victoria signed first and then as Albert took the pen, the duke tried to snatch it from him; there was a tussle which Albert won. Even as an old man, Cumberland, it seems, could cause only trouble.

He died in 1851 and even *The Times* newspaper refused to publish its customary black-edged paper. In its leader, the paper simply said what the nation no doubt felt: 'The good that can be said of the Royal dead is little or none.'

*   *   *

As we descend the ranks of George III's remaining sons we reach a group who had no hope of ever becoming king yet had somehow to fill their time. Perhaps the most eccentric but harmless of this group was Augustus Frederick, Duke of Sussex (1773–1843), the sixth son of George III.

Augustus, like his eldest brother George IV, caused a huge scandal in his youth by marrying a Catholic. However, his

Catholic marriage was declared null and void by George III so he took a mistress and settled down to decades of eccentricity in a vast apartment at Kensington. He collected thousands of clocks and religious manuscripts and invented a chair that enabled him to sleep bolt upright – he later gifted the chair to his brother William. Augustus caused outrage by supporting Catholic emancipation and parliamentary reform. Despite his collection of Bibles, he declared himself entirely unconvinced by any aspect of Christian dogma, least of all the afterlife – which is perhaps why, in an extraordinary break with royal tradition, he left instructions that he should be buried in a municipal cemetery rather than at Windsor.

* * *

The seventh of George III's sons – and the last who survived childhood – was Adolphus, Duke of Cambridge. It has always been a great disappointment to historians that Adolphus appears to have been not in the least bit scandalous. He was, in the words of historian Roger Fulford, 'dutiful, sober [and] moral and honoured his mother and father'.

In fact, so virtuous was Adolphus that he has been almost entirely forgotten by history. He had no political or military interest – apart from a stint in the Hanoverian army – and had none of his brother Augustus's eccentricities (nor his brothers' penchant for Catholic wives).

Born at Buckingham House (now Buckingham Palace) in 1774, he was sent, inevitably, to Germany. In 1801 he was created Duke of Cambridge. Returning to England in 1803, he lived at St James's Palace and at Windsor until 1813 when he returned to Hanover, where he was appointed governor general in 1816.

Like all of George III's sons, the Duke of Cambridge came under pressure to marry and produce an heir. Dutifully, he married Princess Augusta (1797–1889), daughter of the Landgrave of Hesse-Kassell (and perhaps more importantly a great-granddaughter of George II), and in 1819 a child was born, but too late – the Duke of Kent's daughter, Victoria, born in the same year, took precedence. For much of the rest of his life, the Duke of Cambridge remained in Hanover. Returning to England finally in 1837, he found it changed utterly from a country where horse transport dominated to a country where trains now whirled along at more than thirty miles an hour. The duke lived on, scandal free and popular, until 1850.

* * *

The problem that afflicted all the sons of George III except the Prince Regent – with the possible exception of the Duke of Cambridge – was that they hated not being first in line to the throne. Like royal men today, they had nominal military careers but for much of their lives they were idle, rich and obsessed with exercising dictatorial power in their personal lives.

As we have seen throughout royal history, a lack of political power among royal males leads to an intense craving for power and control in the personal sphere – hence the obsessive insistence among all George III's sons on their importance and their right to spend unlimited amounts of money on the grounds, as the Duke of Kent supposedly put it, that 'the country was lucky to have me'.

If the sons of George III were unlikely ever to become king, they would make up for it by ruling their wives and mistresses and having tantrums when Parliament refused to allow them unlimited financial support.

Personal power combined with vast wealth has caused problems for members of the royal family down the ages, but perhaps most especially in the twentieth and twenty-first centuries. Queen Elizabeth II's sister, Princess Margaret, was famously self-indulgent and obsessed with her own importance; she spent wildly, committed adultery and was an alcoholic who was always convinced she would have made a much better queen than her sister. But it was Queen Elizabeth II's second son, Prince Andrew, whose sense of his own importance and high abilities led, as we will see, to one of the greatest royal scandals in history.

CHAPTER NINE

JOHN BROWN'S LEGS: VICTORIA'S SECOND HUSBAND

'The important thing is not what they think of me,
but what I think of them.'

QUEEN VICTORIA

While the vast nineteenth-century underclass lived at a level of poverty unimaginable today, Queen Victoria (1819–1901) amassed more than 300 carriages and had a penchant for champagne. She also insisted on paying £1,200 a year to the Hereditary Grand Falconer despite not owning a single falcon. But this sort of perverse insistence on rewarding aristocrats and relatives for doing nothing had a long history – the Prince Regent, aged twenty-two, insisted that his wet nurse should continue to be paid her annual salary.

There were murmurs of discontent about Victoria's extravagance as there had been about her uncle the Prince Regent's, but it was hardly scandalous. Her foul temper and extraordinary greed also passed largely without comment, but her relationship with her gillie John Brown (1826–83) was perhaps the greatest scandal in an age obsessed with sexual propriety.

It was also a scandal that harked back to ancient rumours that Victoria's mother had also taken a lover – this was the all-controlling Irish aristocrat Sir John Conroy who stalked the corridors of Kensington Palace and utterly dominated Victoria's mother, the Duchess of Kent. Rumour even suggested that Victoria's father was not the sadistic Duke of Kent at all, but Conroy.

No conclusive evidence has been uncovered to indicate the truth or otherwise of the rumour, but Conroy had certainly been close to Victoria's mother during the final years of her husband's life and he moved quickly after the duke's death to consolidate his power over both the duchess and Victoria. And it is certainly true that the court was abuzz with rumours about Victoria's true parentage – rumours that continued for the rest of her life and beyond. According to court diarist Charles Greville, when he was asked directly if he thought Conroy was Victoria's father, the Duke of Wellington replied, 'I suppose so.' Wellington also repeated a widely circulated story that as a young woman Victoria had entered a room at Kensington unexpectedly and found Conroy and her mother in a compromising position. Greville records that Victoria had seen her mother 'engaged in some familiarities', a euphemism for an intimate embrace. Some of these rumours reached Victoria's mother and on one occasion, she was so furious at being challenged directly about her behaviour with Conroy that she dismissed her close adviser Madame de Spaeth. Victoria insisted later in life that her mother was far too pious to have had an affair with Conroy but then Victoria, who was obsessed with sexual propriety, was hardly likely to have thought otherwise.

Conroy was far wilier and more intelligent than the duchess's late husband – he was also extremely manipulative and unscrupulous. After his death it was discovered, for example, that he had stolen large amounts of the duchess's money while they were together at Kensington Palace. But whatever the truth of Victoria's parentage, there is a strong suggestion that Conroy was at the very least the Duchess of Kent's lover after the death of her husband.

Victoria refused to believe the rumours about her mother's affair but she made enormous efforts to distance herself from her dissolute ancestors, especially those wicked uncles. But as we will see, the powerful sexual drive that ran through the Stuarts and the Hanoverians also ran through the Saxe-Coburgs, Victoria especially.

We know that Victoria's passion for Prince Albert (1819–1861) was intensely physical, but that passion was permitted as it was within the bounds of marriage. Victoria's passion for another man, a man considered quite unsuitable for her, was a scandal that rocked the court and outraged the queen's courtiers and ministers. They found themselves forced to be civil at Buckingham Palace and Balmoral Castle to a man they felt was nothing more than a common servant; a man who was doted on by the monarch in whose eyes he could do no wrong.

In fact, Queen Victoria's affair with her gillie John Brown

almost led to a mass resignation of officials. This has long been known, but less well known is the fact that Victoria almost certainly married John Brown and that theirs may well have been a sexual relationship, as we will see.

And Victoria had other scandalous secrets in addition to her affair with Brown. She had long been addicted to opium by the time she met Brown but she came increasingly to rely on it, especially after Brown's death. But opium was a powerful, highly addictive drug – it was essentially heroin. Astonishingly, Queen Victoria's drug use did not stop there – she was also addicted to cocaine. Whenever she met the young Winston Churchill, for example, the two would sit together and talk while chewing gum laced with large quantities of the drug.

After Brown's death, the queen became increasingly reliant on opium. When her doctor advised her not to take so much of the drug, she was furious and, according to historian Roger Fulford, hurled a 'heavy object', probably a paperweight from her desk, at him. Unlike Victoria's daughter Helena, who smoked opium throughout her adult life – through a specially made pipe that looked rather like a miniature hookah – Victoria usually took her opium dissolved in a 90 per cent alcohol mixture. This was laudanum. Given that the effects of laudanum can be maintained only if increasing amounts of the drug are taken, it is probably safe to assume that by the end of her life she was taking the equivalent to a lethal dose for someone who had never taken opium before. Of course, few people would have been scandalised by this at the time as the habit of smoking opium or taking laudanum was extremely common in nineteenth-century

England. Opium seemed a miraculous cure for aches and pains, especially chronic pain and the pain associated with terminal illnesses, such as cancer. Cocaine was equally popular and it continued to be added to many proprietary medicines, even medicines meant for babies and young children, until well into the 1950s – the present writer recalls his mother explaining that she had been advised to buy Daffy's Elixir in the 1950s. It was recommended as the perfect solution to fractious babies, but that was because it contained a small amount of cocaine. It was cocaine from which Coca-Cola got its name and its initial popularity. Bizarrely, cocaine was removed from the drink in 1903 only because the American government was persuaded it made black men want to have sex with white women! Writing in the *New York Times* in 2013, Grace Elizabeth Hale explained:

Anyone with a nickel, black or white, could now drink the cocaine-infused beverage. Middle-class whites worried that soft drinks were contributing to what they saw as exploding cocaine use among African-Americans. Southern newspapers reported that 'negro cocaine fiends' were raping white women, the police powerless to stop them. By 1903, [then manager of Coca-Cola Asa Griggs] Candler had bowed to white fears (and a wave of anti-narcotics legislation), removing the cocaine and adding more sugar and caffeine.

The great question then and now is how on earth did John Brown become such a great favourite with Victoria who was notoriously bad-tempered and deeply snobbish?

The clue lies in Brown's character and in Victoria's need for someone who did not always defer to her as everyone else – even her children – did. Brown often treated her with disdain; he would scold her and lose his temper and she loved it.

Brown was born in Crathienaird, Aberdeenshire in 1826. By the time he had reached his early twenties he was working at Balmoral as a gillie – the word 'gillie' comes from the Gaelic word for a servant working predominantly outside, but is associated now with deer stalking and fishing. If you want to shoot a deer in Scotland or fish for salmon you might well be accompanied by a gillie even today. At the time Brown began to work at Balmoral, the house and estate were owned not by the queen, but by Lord Aberdeen's brother.

Victoria and Albert had been visiting the estate since 1848 when Brown was twenty-two, and in 1852 they bought it. John Brown and Balmoral were to become almost synonymous with Victoria's ideal of happiness.

Victoria and Albert took possession of Old Balmoral Castle, a sixteenth-century house that they soon decided was far too small for their needs so they commissioned a new residence, which was completed in 1856. The old house was far more attractive to modern eyes than the heavy, lumpen Scottish baronial building that replaced it – the Balmoral we see today – but Victoria loved her new house and the vast estate that surrounded it; today amounting to around 50,000 acres. Albert loved the house because the surrounding hills reminded him of Germany but both Victoria and Albert were agreed that, as Victoria noted in her journal, it was the 'freedom and peace' of the estate that lay at the heart of its appeal. Others were not so sure. Visitors found the house cold and gloomy. Biographer A. N. Wilson quotes Foreign Secretary Lord Stanley's astonishment during a visit to Balmoral at the queen's 'love of exposure to the weather and her dislike of heat'. He thought her liking for the dark cold rooms 'almost morbid'.

There is no evidence that Victoria paid much attention to Brown before the death of her husband in 1861, but she enjoyed his company when riding on her favourite pony.

Despite the precarious nature of life in nineteenth-century England, even for members of the royal family, the shock of Albert's death aged just forty-two never really left Victoria. She went into a period of deep mourning that lasted for the rest of her long life. She liked people to think that both Albert and her marriage to him had been perfect in every way, but in fact their relationship had been stormy to say the least – they had rowed regularly, screamed insults at each other and often sulked for days on end refusing to speak to each other.

The unique circumstances of being married to the Queen of England meant Albert could not take the lead role as every other husband in the country was assumed to do, and he hated it. He pushed continually to be allowed more responsibility for the limited powers the monarch still enjoyed, but Victoria enjoyed wielding these powers far too much to allow this.

Having been deferred to throughout her adult life after she had assumed the throne, it seems that Victoria partly enjoyed these rows – it was as if they added spice to her relationship with Albert, and she missed them when he died; there was something in her that enjoyed being told what to do by a man. None of her ministers would dare be anything other than diplomatic and deferential to her – even when they felt she was behaving atrociously (or unconstitutionally), they would merely remonstrate politely. John Brown, a man as traditional in his outlook and attitudes as Prince Albert, was very different.

Following Albert's death, Victoria developed a great liking for the straight-talking Brown. So much so that Brown was with Victoria during a carriage outing from Buckingham Palace to Regent's Park in 1872. As the carriage returned to the palace, Brown spotted a young man – later identified as Arthur O'Connor – who had sneaked around to the garden entrance to the palace and was now within a few feet of the queen. O'Connor was holding what looked like a loaded gun. The quick-thinking Brown rushed at O'Connor and pinned him to the ground until the police arrived. O'Connor had a history of mental illness and the gun he was carrying turned out, according to Victoria's biographer A. N. Wilson, to be loaded with nothing more than wads of paper. He was sentenced to twenty lashes with the birch and a year's hard labour; the queen protested that this was far too lenient. But Brown's actions confirmed his heroic status in the queen's eyes and he was awarded the Devoted Service Medal.

Brown's courage confirmed a deep affection in the queen that lasted right up to his death in 1883. The secret of Brown's hold over the queen was that he treated her as an ordinary woman. It was the fact that he was not an aristocrat used to the ways of the court that made him so appealing. He was refreshingly different and refreshingly masculine. His no-nonsense attitude to her and his scoldings were seen as shockingly rude by the court, but Victoria enjoyed her advisers' shock as much as she enjoyed the fact that Brown treated them with barely disguised contempt.

Brown's relationship with Victoria developed to the point where it threatened to become a serious constitutional issue, an issue over which senior figures were prepared publicly to resign. The relationship was the talk of the court for years, but every attempt to warn Victoria that her behaviour was unseemly or inappropriate brought merely a storm of anger.

She seemed at times to go out of her way to annoy her courtiers by promoting Brown and taking him with her wherever she went. His bluntness with her increased, but he also joked and teased which endeared him even further to her. Though serious herself, she loved jokes and teasing.

She made sure Brown attended the anniversary of Prince Albert's death each year at Windsor Castle and demanded he accompany her on public appearances. He became a regular feature marching behind her coach each time she set off from Buckingham Palace, in the full Highland dress she, rather eccentrically, insisted on him wearing.

It was even rumoured that the queen had become convinced Brown wasn't Brown at all – that he was a human figure in which the spirit of her late husband had taken up residence. Victoria's ideas about Brown embodying the spirit of Albert were part of what came to be a national obsession with ghosts, spirits and the paranormal. By the end of the century, seances were being held in towns, cities and villages across the country. It is perhaps no coincidence that belief in the spirit world grew in the decades following the publication of Charles Darwin's 1859 book *On the Origin of Species*, a work which made some Christians doubt or even reject their faith. This led to an upsurge of interest in alternative routes to what was often described as the spirit world.

An extract from the queen's own diary shows the depth of her feeling for Brown: 'Often I told him no one loved him more than I did or had a better friend than me: and he answered "Nor you – than me. No one loves you more."' It was his sheer masculinity that entranced her: 'Brown with his strong, powerful arm, helped me along wonderfully.'

Brown became the focus of massive rage and discontent – the aristocrats, the barons of old, who were closest to the queen and felt a proprietorial interest in her were certainly jealous of Brown's influence and there was a good deal of snobbery involved. Brown, they insisted, was not a gentleman. Brown was a servant. Brown was common.

Rumours began to circulate that Victoria might even be sleeping with Brown – a not unreasonable speculation given what was later to transpire, and it was known that Victoria was remarkably uninhibited when it came to the pleasures of the flesh: she loved eating and drinking and she was decidedly uninhibited with her husband.

Many historians and biographers have emphasised that, judging by her letters and journals, Victoria delighted in her physical relationship with Albert and was not in the least repressed. After her first night as Albert's wife she wrote in her journal:

It was a gratifying and bewildering experience ... I never, never spent such an evening. His excessive love and affection gave me feelings of heavenly love and happiness. He clasped me in his arms and we kissed each other again and again.

His beauty, his sweetness and gentleness – really how can I ever be thankful enough to have such a husband!

To lie by his side, and in his arms, and on his dear bosom, and be called by names of tenderness, I have never yet heard used to me before – this was the happiest day of my life. It was bliss beyond belief!

When day dawned (for we did not sleep much) and I beheld that beautiful face by my side, it was more than I can express! Oh, was ever woman so blessed as I am.

A few months later Albert sent her an erotic statue of himself as a half-naked Greek warrior. He quickly decided it was too risqué to be on display and had it hidden away. A more decorous copy was commissioned and remains at Buckingham Palace today.

Victoria saw Brown very much as a replacement for Albert and there is reason to suppose he was to replace Albert everywhere, including in Victoria's bed. But Brown had powerful enemies who were determined to be rid of him – their feelings were no doubt not dissimilar to those of the barons who surrounded Edward II and were equally determined to be rid of Piers Gaveston.

As A. N. Wilson points out in *Victoria: A Life*, Brown's greatest enemy was General Charles Grey who compared Victoria's self-indulgence with her son the Prince of Wales, 'a notorious womaniser'. Grey became so obsessed with Brown that he and other courtiers put it about that Brown might even be a threat to the monarchy. They knew this was nonsense but no doubt hoped it would get back to Victoria and she would act, which perhaps shows how little they knew their queen.

It is not difficult to believe that Victoria enjoyed her courtiers' discomfiture at her love for Brown and love is certainly not too strong a word for their relationship – at one point she was even copying Brown's mannerisms, she drank whisky with him and she could hardly bear to spend a day without seeing him. If this was not love – with a large element of sexual attraction – then what was it?

But the ultimate scandal of their relationship was revealed only in a deathbed confession. A. N. Wilson takes up the story. On 17 February 1885, he explains, 'Lewis Harcourt [son of Gladstone's Home Secretary] wrote that Lady Ponsonby – wife of the Queen's private secretary – "told the Home Secretary a few days ago that Miss Macleod declares that her brother Norman Macleod confessed to her on his deathbed that he had married the Queen to John Brown".'

The story has never been confirmed but it would not have surprised many of those who knew Victoria well. Like her Hanoverian ancestors, especially her wicked uncles, Victoria felt that in the private sphere she could do as she pleased; her view was that a queen could not be told what she could and could not do. It is perhaps likely that Victoria's belief that Albert had somehow come to inhabit John Brown also made her feel that there was nothing at all inappropriate about the idea of going through some sort of marriage ceremony. It may well have been a simple blessing of some kind conducted by Norman Macleod, a blessing that would have seemed a private and personal matter to the queen and one that answered to her need to formally link herself to Brown. What is certain is that no clergyman would have lied during a deathbed confession.

Victoria modified her behaviour only when she was on the very brink of what the courtiers knew would be a scandal to end all scandals.

In 1868 Victoria published *Leaves from the Journal of Our Life in the Highlands, from 1848 to 1861* and in 1884 she published *More Leaves from the Journal of Our Life in the Highlands, from 1862 to 1882.* Though today both books seem anodyne to the point of unreadability, they were popular at the time.

When Victoria, who believed she had real talent as a writer, published her first book in 1868 it was dedicated to Prince Albert but those who read with care realised that the real subject of that first book was Brown. The dedication to Albert seems to have allayed any fears that Brown was seen as anything more than a loyal servant. But Victoria's family were not fooled and all of her children, especially the Prince of Wales, were hurt and angry. But if her children were upset at their mother's first foray into print, they were in for an even greater shock. Her third book was to be a complete and intimate account of her love and admiration for Brown. Victoria's family, ministers and advisers were appalled – a relationship they considered inappropriate was about to be described in detail for anyone and everyone to read. The queen would be a laughing stock, not just in Britain but across the British Empire.

Victoria showed the manuscript of her third volume to the Dean of Windsor. The dean was so shocked by what he read that he could hardly speak. Part of his shock stemmed from something he already knew that the queen did not. Isolated from the world in her ivory towered palaces, Victoria was unaware that a perceptive world had already guessed that she had a passion for John Brown, and in America – where the press had a habit of printing material that would have been suppressed in England – a satirical pamphlet had recently been published under the title *John Brown's Legs*. The tone of the booklet can be judged by just one line – a line where the queen is purported to say, 'Have written a note to Tennyson commanding him to write a sonnet on John Brown's legs.'

The anonymous author was nearer the mark than they could ever have imagined when they wrote their skit, because the queen really had complimented Brown on his legs on many occasions and in the hearing of her courtiers.

Despite moments of self-awareness, the queen generally assumed that if she thought something was right and proper then it must be so. When she was told Brown was unpopular, she dismissed this as nonsense. When she was told Brown was an unsuitable companion, she assumed that his critics were simply jealous of him. When the Dean of Windsor gently suggested it might be inappropriate to publish her third volume of memoirs with its open confession of her adoration of Brown, Victoria stamped her foot and raged at him. The dean felt powerless to do more but was unwilling to face the storm he felt would engulf him if the third volume really did reach the public, so he told the queen that if she went ahead with publication, he would be forced to resign. Taken aback, Victoria insisted the dean must apologise for suggesting there was any comparison to be made between writing about her late husband and writing about Brown. Stalemate ensued, but the queen had a moment of realisation and – rarely for her – backed down. Volume three, the great love letter to Brown, vanished and was almost certainly destroyed.

It is possible a copy remains somewhere hidden away in Windsor Castle, but if it has survived it would be remarkable, especially as, after his mother's death, the Prince of Wales, Edward VII from 1901, did as much as he could to destroy all evidence of her connection with Brown – burning her papers, destroying photographs and mementoes and removing statues. It is ironic that Edward VII, one of the most scandalous monarchs in history, should have been so sensitive about his mother's own little indiscretions. Perhaps it was more his mother's final wishes that caused the most upset: she was buried with Brown's mother's wedding ring, a handkerchief he had once owned and a photograph of him. At Victoria's very last moment, Albert, it seems, was forgotten.

CHAPTER TEN

HELL-BENT ON PLEASURE:
EDWARD VII'S 'LOOSE BOX'

'Now at least I know where he is.'

QUEEN ALEXANDRA ON THE DEATH OF HER HUSBAND EDWARD VII

Edward VII (1841–1910), known to his friends as Bertie, is the only British monarch to have both been born and died at Buckingham Palace. By the time he was born in 1841, the palace had been the centre of court life since George III's accession in 1760. Originally known as Buckingham House, it was built in 1703 for John Sheffield, Duke of Buckingham. Enlarged and remodelled repeatedly, the palace has changed out of all recognition, but it is an extraordinary building with 775 rooms, a 39-acre garden, a near forty-metre ballroom and 188 rooms just for staff. In the seventeenth century, the marshy site on which the palace stands had been a mulberry garden fed by the Tyburn Brook, which still runs under the forecourt. Under Edward's mother, Queen Victoria, the original three-winged house had become the vast courtyard house we see today with its dramatic east front facing along the Mall. Curiously, much of the mid-Victorian work on Buckingham Palace was carried out by Thomas Cubitt, the great-great-great-grandfather of Camilla, Duchess of Cornwall, herself no stranger to scandal.

Determined that Edward should be a serious, intellectual monarch, Albert devised a rigid, extremely demanding regime of study for his son. This began when Bertie was a little over seven and it was a hopeless endeavour from the start. Bertie's biographer Jane Ridley explains: 'Albert engaged a tutor named Henry Birch … He was installed next door to Bertie's room at Buckingham Palace, and Albert drew up a syllabus and timetable. The first few weeks were disastrous. Bertie was rude, disobedient and rebellious.'

Albert decided Bertie should be whipped. From then on whenever he disobeyed, he was whipped and whipped again; he never became the serious intellectual his father had wanted him to be. Victoria stayed in the background, expressing her occasional disgust at her son's lack of progress. Bertie never liked Buckingham Palace, the scene of these early humiliations, but the palace was off-putting in other ways: it became gloomy and grubby after his mother's long reign and refusal to change anything. She had preferred Windsor and Balmoral, but Buckingham Palace had the same depressing stamp of mourning that afflicted all her residences.

Agnes Cook began work in the palace kitchens shortly after the death of Queen Victoria and she remembered:

dark clutter everywhere, and the rooms none too clean, but then it was almost impossible to keep them clean despite all the maids. The windows too were filthy so the interiors looked even worse than they might have done. Plaster seemed to be coming off the walls too and the gilded walls and furniture all looked faded. I think it was because Victoria wanted to keep the palace as much as possible as it had been when her husband was alive. But the new king [Edward VII] hated all that and had a big clear out as I think he did at Windsor and Balmoral.

*　　*　　*

After his unhappy childhood, it is perhaps understandable that Edward VII both during his reign and while he was the Prince of Wales should have led a life that, for an ordinary person, might well have resulted in a prison sentence.

Perjury then as now was a serious criminal offence almost invariably punished by a custodial sentence and Edward certainly committed perjury at least once with regard to one of his mistresses, possibly on more occasions. He was also a thief who could not resist stealing from his friends' houses and he was prepared to lie to punish a former friend who had slept with his mistress, Daisy Brooke.

From the time he was aware of anything at all, Edward would have been aware that his mother's main interest in life was to remind him that he could never hope to be as good or intelligent a man as his father, Prince Albert. In a letter to her eldest daughter Victoria, always known as Vicky, Queen Victoria describes her daughters as 'nicer' and her son Edward as 'frightful'.

She also confessed in a letter to Vicky that she had direct contact with her younger children only 'once every three months'. She loathed the whole idea of motherhood and babies. Breastfeeding was her greatest horror. When she heard her daughters had chosen to breastfeed their own children, she said, 'It makes my hair stand on end that my daughters have turned into cows.'

Frustrated by his continual sense that he could never please his mother, Edward determined that as soon as he could escape, he would do so and would do as he pleased. Once out of the schoolroom, he vowed never again to read a book or study anything.

His whole adult life was to be devoted to eating, drinking, smoking and sleeping with other men's wives. Of course, rumours of his lifestyle reached his mother's ears as early as 1859–60 while he was still a student, and she redoubled her efforts to tell him how much of a disappointment he was. Inevitably, this had the opposite effect from the one intended and Bertie became ever more debauched. Things reached a peak when Prince Albert visited his son at Cambridge, where he was ostensibly studying, to remonstrate with him about his bad habits. The two men went for a walk, it rained, Albert returned to Windsor, caught a chill and died.

For the rest of her life Victoria insisted that Bertie was responsible for his father's premature death. In fact, Albert was already ill when he visited his son in Cambridge and the real cause of his death was typhoid. Victoria refused to believe it.

Bertie rarely criticised his mother in public, although according to historian A. N. Wilson, towards the end of her life, he quipped: 'Most people pray to the Eternal Father, but I am the only one afflicted with an Eternal Mother.'

But if Bertie loathed his mother, the feeling was mutual. She wrote to her daughter saying that she could never look at Bertie 'without a shudder'. She had watched poor Albert, she said, struck down and get worse day by day before he finally died. 'I doubt whether you could bear the sight of the one who was the cause.'

Queen Victoria's intense dislike of her son and heir is a remarkable echo of the extraordinarily dysfunctional relationships between all the British monarchs of the eighteenth century and their first-born sons; though Victoria was a Saxe-Coburg she was also, of course, a Hanoverian, being the granddaughter of George III.

These deep antagonistic feelings between Victoria and her eldest son meant that, until the end of her life, Victoria refused to allow Bertie any involvement in the day-to-day work of the monarch. As a result, when he came to the throne in 1901 – he had been the Prince of Wales for sixty years – he was wholly unprepared, but, ironically, this is where his love of wine and women (and tobacco) stood him in good stead. He quickly decided – sensibly, given his hatred of work – to allow his ministers to do their work with no interference from him. This was very different from his mother's approach. It was a classic case of making a virtue (or in his case, complete lack of virtue) of necessity. His mother had interfered, scolded and nagged her ministers. Bertie did the opposite and the government of the day must have been absolutely delighted.

And there were other contrasts between Bertie and his mother that made him very popular with the public.

During her long widowhood, Victoria had occasionally refused to open Parliament; she was aloof, permanently gloomy and disliked crowds. Bertie once again was entirely the opposite: he made it clear that the age of austerity was over; he embodied the public's desire for fun and indulgence after the long years when fun was made to seem immoral. Victoria's baleful influence on the country can be judged by the fact that black became almost the only colour a gentleman could wear. This was in stark contrast to the bright colours worn by gentlemen during the Regency and the reign of William IV. Even interior design was affected by the general atmosphere of gloom – black slate clocks were made in their millions, for example, far exceeding the number of clocks made in brass and other, brighter materials. Funerals became absurdly elaborate. There was almost, it seemed to some, a cult of death as funeral monuments became ever more elaborate. A leader in the *Kensington News and West London Times* in November 1890 complained that many monuments in Kensal Green cemetery were 'bigger and more elaborate than people's houses'.

Life had become one long dirge which meant that Bertie could behave as outrageously as he pleased and the public would forgive him. And outrageous is probably far too mild a word for what Bertie got up to.

While his wife Alexandra (1844–1925) was, to use Bertie's own words, his 'brood mare', he spent as much of his time as possible with a series of mistresses, most famously Alice Keppel

(1868–1947). Continuing the horse metaphor, he described them as his 'loose box'. What was extraordinary about his relationship with Mrs Keppel – and with the actor Lillie Langtry, not to mention countless aristocratic wives including Jennie Churchill, mother of the more famous Winston – was that he carried on the affair largely in public. He would leave Buckingham Palace with Mrs Keppel and visit the theatre; as they left the theatre at the end of the evening, they were frequently cheered by the crowd. The public might have paid lip service to the sort of family values Queen Victoria had espoused, but as in every age there was another life beneath the surface of respectability and Bertie embodied that life in his drinking and womanising. He became what his ancestor Charles II had been to the 1660s and what pop stars were in the 1960s: a symbol of hedonistic freedom. But Bertie was also a throwback to Victoria's wicked uncles; like the Prince Regent and his brothers, Bertie cared for nothing but his own pleasure and was prepared to lie and cheat to get his way. Each time he cheated or lied, he relied on the respect paid to his position as the Prince of Wales to save him from scandal, but it did not always work.

The curious morality of aristocratic and royal life in the early twentieth century meant that it was acceptable for Bertie to commit adultery, but quite unacceptable for him to cheat at cards. Yet Bertie's determination to get his way led to an incident which damaged his reputation and led to him appearing in court, an appearance that caused his mother to threaten never to speak to him again.

The incident that sparked the wholly sorry business occurred in 1890 during a game of baccarat at Tranby Croft, the Yorkshire home of Bertie's ship-owning friend Arthur Wilson. The nub of the story is that Bertie almost certainly invented an accusation of cheating at cards after discovering that his friend the soldier and millionaire landowner Sir William Gordon-Cumming was sleeping with Bertie's mistress, Daisy Brooke. By accusing him of cheating, Bertie clearly hoped that Gordon-Cumming would be shunned by society.

Few believed Bertie's assertion that Gordon-Cumming had cheated at cards. He was descended from one of Britain's most ancient families and was used to losing large sums at cards – money he could easily afford.

Hints of a deep conspiratorial scandal began soon after the alleged incident. It seems that Gordon-Cumming was threatened with public exposure if he did not agree to sign a guarantee that he would never play cards again. That agreement was to be witnessed by all those present. Faced with this threat, Gordon-Cumming signed, but within weeks he had begun a legal action to sue all those present at the card game – an astonishingly risky act if he really had been guilty of cheating.

A legal action such as this between a group of aristocrats obsessed with their honour and dignity might have gone unnoticed but for one thing: Gordon-Cumming's legal team insisted on calling the Prince of Wales as a witness.

Palace officials did their best to stop the story reaching the newspapers, but they had reckoned without the Prince of Wales's erstwhile mistress Daisy Brooke, a notorious gossip whose nickname, appropriately enough, was 'Babbling Brooke'. Daisy delighted in the story and spread it far and wide.

When news of the case reached Queen Victoria she was horrified. For any member of her family, let alone the heir to the throne, to be called as a witness in such a case was deeply dishonourable, but then she would no doubt have reflected that Bertie was merely confirming once again what she had always thought of him: he was a reprobate who brought nothing but shame on the royal family.

It was no doubt partly the dread of the inevitable interview with his mother that prompted Bertie to do his best behind the scenes to stop Gordon-Cumming's action before it ever reached court, but Gordon-Cumming would not be persuaded.

In the end, Gordon-Cumming lost the case because the judge simply could not countenance the idea that the heir to the throne might be a liar.

It is widely accepted now, as A. N. Wilson points out in *Victoria: A Life*, that it was actually Bertie who had cheated at cards. The accusation of cheating had been thrown on to Gordon-Cumming to protect the prince. In his evidence Bertie insisted that Gordon-Cumming had cheated and by doing so the heir to the throne committed perjury, an act for which he should have gone to prison. But in condemning Gordon-Cumming, Bertie could not avoid incriminating himself. Gambling was illegal at this time in Britain and Bertie was forced to admit he had been gambling.

*　　*　　*

Perhaps the greatest scandal of Bertie's life had occurred many years earlier when he had been forced into the witness box in a divorce case – with his penchant for other men's wives, this was always a theoretical risk, but Bertie expected the unwritten code of the aristocracy to prevail, especially given that he would have assumed that all his friends were sleeping with each other's wives.

The general promiscuity of the aristocracy during this period is well attested by numerous memoirs. Dolly West's mother, Gladys, worked as a maid at a number of big country houses from 1906 to 1926 and she recalled what she described as the 'goings-on' of a typical aristocratic weekend:

My mother used to say that Bertie cared about only one thing – he was hell-bent on pleasure. That's what his country house weekends were about. The guests always had an air about them when they arrived. It was as if they knew they were the most important people on earth. They had a rigid code of behaviour with each other and with us servants because they had never lived without people to light their fires, run their baths, cook their food or wash their clothes. They were like babies – couldn't do a thing for themselves. And they were bored. In the servants' hall we used to joke about what they got up to at night. The butler used to tell us that certain guests had to have bedrooms close to certain other guests so that the various couples could swap wives! We girls couldn't believe it, especially when the butler told us King Edward would sometimes change bedrooms twice in a night!

*   *   *

Bertie's affairs inevitably began in the same way. Whenever he wanted to sleep with a married woman, he would befriend her husband and begin showering both husband and wife with gifts. He would then get his equerry Francis Knollys to arrange a visit.

The preparations for Bertie's afternoon visits were always the same. They were witnessed by 22-year-old Elsie Gill who told the story towards the end of her life to the writer Anita Leslie.

Elsie describes how, on the day of the king's visit, the maids were instructed to fill the room with flowers and spray it heavily with scent. The curtains were then discreetly drawn. The servants were given strict instructions to stay out of the way when the door was locked at the appointed hour. Bertie always tried to ensure no one saw him actually visit any of his numerous lady friends; again, a protocol insisted on by Francis Knollys – 'the king's pimp' as one servant, Agnes Cook, described him. The elaborate preparations were designed to create what the king saw as a seductive atmosphere.

In her unpublished memoir, Agnes Cook confirms the description of these preparations given by Elsie Gill:

The curtains were drawn in the drawing room perhaps half an hour before the king was due to arrive and the king himself always sent flowers on ahead so the room would be full of blooms – sometimes hundreds of them. And scent was sprinkled everywhere so the smell was almost overpowering. It was like a code – any woman who agreed to an unchaperoned visit that was preceded by notes and instructions from Knollys and flowers from the king knew also that sex was expected.

To reduce the chances of a public scandal, Bertie would often find a way to pay a great deal of money to the husband of some-one he was determined to sleep with. He might find lucrative employment for the husband or discreetly pay him off through an intermediary. In return for not making a fuss, for example, Alice Keppel's husband benefited from both the large amounts of money and jewellery Edward gave to Keppel's wife and a well-paid job that involved very little work.

Lady Mordaunt's husband was the first to make a major public fuss about his wife's affair with the prince. This was a serious breach of the aristocratic code of silence. When Mordaunt discovered his wife's infidelity, he was furious, especially when he discovered that she had been sleeping with the Prince of Wales and two other members of their circle. Mordaunt sued for divorce but in a manner that partly paid heed to the rules of the game, he cited only Lord Cole and Sir Frederick Johnstone as co-respondents, not the Prince of Wales. There is no doubt he was furious with Bertie but Bertie was the Prince of Wales and even Mordaunt baulked at the idea of dragging him through the courts.

Bertie ran his relationships and his circle of friends much as a mafia godfather might run his. The prince was powerful but he also had powerful friends and Mordaunt was heavily encouraged to try to keep the prince out of the whole sordid business. Truth did not matter; princes were above the law. But in this instance no amount of behind-the-scenes bullying could keep Bertie entirely out of the case. Word quickly spread that the Prince of Wales was involved. Rumours circulated widely and as a result Bertie was finally forced to give evidence when the case came to trial in 1870. No Prince of Wales had appeared in court in such a fashion since the early fifteenth century and it is easy to imagine how horrified Queen Victoria must have been.

In the witness box, Bertie was treated with absurd deference – he was not cross-examined and the judge's summing up was blatantly biased in his favour. Bertie admitted he had visited Lady Mordaunt in her husband's absence on numerous occasions, but flatly denied there had been any impropriety. In this he certainly committed perjury for it was an accepted fact in Victorian England that, in the absence of her husband, a man did not visit a woman to whom he was not married and spend time with her alone and with the curtains drawn. And throughout Bertie's long philandering career, it was widely known that his modus operandi with all his mistresses was to visit them when their husbands were away, just as he had visited Lady Mordaunt. The idea that he visited her while her husband was away simply to enjoy her conversation was ridiculed.

The extent to which the establishment connived to ensure the prince was protected can be perhaps best judged by the fact that when Bertie approached the eminent lawyer and Chief Justice for the Queen's Bench Sir Alexander Cockburn for advice, he was told that if a woman had given herself to a man, that man was obliged to protect her honour even if that involved committing perjury.

Perhaps the most deeply shocking thing about the trial was that it was decided that Lady Mordaunt was mad and could not therefore instruct a lawyer to conduct her defence. The case was dismissed and Lady Mordaunt was forced to spend the rest of her life in an asylum. It was a neat if ruthless manoeuvre to ensure no divorce took place. And if there was no divorce, it could not be said that the Prince of Wales had been involved in a divorce.

But this is just the tip of Bertie's scandalous iceberg. Other scandals are almost too numerous to mention: he enjoyed an estimated fifty liaisons of one kind or another with various women over his lifetime; he invited a prostitute called Nellie Clifden to a party at Windsor (some accounts say that, although he invited a prostitute, it was not Nellie); he was blackmailed by a Mr Green whose wife he had seduced – Mr and Mrs Green were paid an annuity of £60 and packed off to New Zealand; and according to former domestic servant Agnes Cook, several of whose family members worked at Buckingham Palace, despite his taste for high-born women, Bertie made a Buckingham Palace maid pregnant. Through an intermediary, she was paid a considerable sum, packed off to her parents in the countryside and told that any mention of Bertie's involvement would lead to prosecution and a prison sentence.

* * *

At the other extreme from public and highly damaging scandals, Bertie found it difficult to do the right thing even when a relatively trivial issue was involved. He always refused to pay speeding tickets, for example, and insisted he should not need to have number plates on his cars. Adrian Tinniswood, in *Behind the Throne: A Domestic History of the British Royal Household*, explains:

> In spite of the fact that the Motor Car Act of 1903 stipulated that all cars on public roads should display vehicle registration plates, none of the King's did so, a practice which frequently led to them being flagged down by irate police officers whose determination to tear a strip off the driver evaporated when they recognised (or worse, didn't recognise and had to be told) the identity of the passenger.

In this respect as in so many others, Bertie embodied a theme that runs back to the earliest days of the struggle between Parliament and monarch to decide who has ultimate control. Bertie knew more than any previous monarch that he had no real political power so he ruthlessly exerted his power in his personal life even when the matter involved was trivial – if he wanted to drive without plates, he would; if he wanted to sleep with another man's wife, he would; if he wanted a good cigarette case he had seen at a friend's house, he would just take it. At the personal level he was a despot: in Edward, the divine right of kings had become debased into the divine right of self-indulgence.

CHAPTER ELEVEN

BROTHEL CREEPERS:
PRINCE EDDY AND
THE BOYS

'The louder he talked of his honour, the faster we counted our spoons.'
RALPH WALDO EMERSON

Queen Victoria's obsession with sexual propriety, an obsession that was, as we have seen, a reaction to the adultery
and promiscuity of her Hanoverian ancestors, inevitably damaged the lives of her children and even, one might argue, her
grandchildren. Horribly repressed by a world that officially refused to accept the existence of sexual passion, the descendants
of Victoria sneaked out of their royal palaces whenever they
could to satisfy a need that simply could not be denied.

It is almost true to say that, officially, for the genteel Victorian, sex simply didn't exist. For women, things were even worse
and the ideal to which they were meant to aspire – a sort of holy
spirit existence – had nothing to do with flesh and blood. This
meant that, unless they were poor and working class, women

were not supposed to work under any circumstances since their pure spirits might be sullied by contact with the sordid world of commerce – they were supposed to embody a weak, delicate ideal of soft womanhood which allowed their husbands to be tough, worldly breadwinners who fantasised about their ability to protect their women from anything in the least unseemly, including sex. Indeed, the delicate ideal woman was not supposed to enjoy sex at all – as part of some strange Victorian fantasy, she was supposed to be above such bestial things and to submit to her husband's animal instincts merely to be able to have children. With this in mind, the old joke about the Victorians covering table legs is hardly a joke at all.

But beneath this absurd artificial construct, there was unavoidably a dark undercurrent that allowed inevitable sexual desire to find an outlet. The obsession with respectability and with keeping sex at bay led to terrible abuses – girls and boys as young as eight could be bought in London's Haymarket on a Saturday night and it was widely known they were being bought for sex. Yet when W. T. Stead, the editor of the *Pall Mall Gazette*, bought a girl to prove that it could easily be done, he was prosecuted and sent to prison for three months. Convicted for drawing attention to the very practice it was claimed did not exist, his offence was actually far more about bringing Victorian society into disrepute. That, not the sale of children, was the unforgivable offence.

If heterosexual sex was a problem whose publicly acceptable solution could be found only in marriage – and even that perhaps grudgingly – how much greater a problem was it for those attracted to members of the same sex? If there was no outlet for young heterosexual women, things were far worse for well-bred young gay men and women.

There were, no doubt, as many gay individuals in Victorian England as there have been in any age and a major part of the London underworld catered for them. There were numerous gay brothels where men and boys could be bought or to which men could bring men they had picked up in the street. The most notorious of these gay brothels was at No. 19 Cleveland Street in London's Bloomsbury. Among those who worked as prostitutes at Cleveland Street, there were boys who, by today's standards at least, were little more than children. In essence, the scandal of the Cleveland Street brothel boils down to a story about sex and corruption in high places. It is yet one more example of how the rich and powerful in Victorian Britain were treated very differently from the poor.

Though it has never been proved conclusively, circumstantial evidence suggests that one of Cleveland Street's customers was Prince Albert Victor (1864–92), who was known as Eddy, Queen Victoria's grandson and the eldest son of the Prince of Wales, later Edward VII. But before we look at whether it is likely that Eddy was in the habit of sneaking out of Buckingham Palace and heading off to Cleveland Street (which was little more than a mile to the north), it's worth taking a brief look at the background to the scandal.

Male brothels existed in London and elsewhere simply because there was a demand for them. Apart from the potential guilt and shame attached to the knowledge that one was attracted to men, there was the risk of prosecution if one attempted to do anything about it. The police deliberately set traps for men and the penalties – as Oscar Wilde was to discover – were severe if you were caught soliciting or engaging in homosexual acts. But whatever the risks, the demand was never going to go away. As a result, houses were set up by the enterprising where men could meet other men safely and discreetly – or at least that was the plan. So long as no one found out what was going on, all was well.

Charles Hammond, the son of a Thames waterman, was the man behind the Cleveland Street brothel. Though barely literate, he was highly intelligent and shrewd.

Hammond had married a French prostitute and was living in Oxenden Street in London's West End earning his living as a male prostitute when he met a young Irish boy called Jack Saul – probably not his real name – who also worked as a prostitute. The two became acquainted and Hammond realised that working as a pimp with a group of boys including Jack was going to make him far richer than working the streets alone. Hammond did not, so far as we know, coerce boys into working for him. Indeed, for many, working at Cleveland Street was seen as an easy way to make far more money than a young man could ever hope to make doing anything else. At some point Jack Saul and a number of other young men began working for Hammond. But they needed a base.

Hammond, now in his mid-thirties, was probably paid by a number of aristocrats with whom he regularly had sex to set up his brothel. It was certainly in their interest to eliminate as much of the risk of arrest as they could and being able to take men back to a safe house for sex rather than having sex in Hyde Park or elsewhere outdoors would have seemed a godsend and worth the few hundred pounds it cost to buy 19 Cleveland Street and install Hammond.

Hammond did so well at Cleveland Street that he was able to furnish the house with fine furniture and pictures, Dresden china and large potted plants – the idea was that it should look like a respectable middle-class household so that anyone who knocked on the door by chance and saw into the hall would see nothing amiss. There were one or two eccentric touches – numerous caged birds and lapdogs, apparently gifts to Hammond from grateful customers – but nothing to suggest the real business being carried on at the address.

As the years passed, Hammond became moderately wealthy. He had beautiful gilt-edged cards printed suggesting all were welcome to this special club. Customers were encouraged to take away a few cards and hand them on to like-minded friends.

By now Hammond's clients included numerous English aristocrats such as Lord Euston and George Cavendish-Bentinck MP, a descendant of the Dukes of Portland, one of whose daughters was to become godmother to Her Royal Highness the late Queen Mother. The irony is that despite his taste for young boys, Cavendish-Bentinck was a staunch supporter of Henry Labouchère whose Criminal Law Amendment Act of 1885 made all homosexual acts between men seriously criminal. Before the 1885 Act, only what was then termed 'buggery' was a criminal offence. Any other physical or sexual acts between men were not, strictly speaking, illegal. Labouchère changed all that.

Another enthusiastic user of Hammond's services was Sir Henry Montague Hozier MP. Sir Henry was later to have his own brother committed to an asylum for having disgraced the family by being seen on friendly terms with two private soldiers – of course, the subtext was that John Hozier was having a sexual relationship with one or both private soldiers, but this could never be admitted. Instead, it was stated that the reason for John Hozier's incarceration was that he must be mad to allow himself, an aristocrat, to be seen shaking hands with a common soldier.

The list of Hammond's upper-class clients became ever longer as time passed, and by the time the house was finally put under surveillance by the police even the false names Hammond's customers adopted did not stop a number of them being identified.

The system at Cleveland Street was that a gentleman would arrive with another man – either a boy or sometimes a guardsman. They would be admitted and offered champagne (if they were sufficiently lordly) and then asked if they would like some privacy. That was code for, 'Would you like to use one of our bedrooms?'

One of Jack Saul's customers at Cleveland Street was Lord Euston, the eldest son of the Duke of Grafton. Saul was able to describe him in great detail to the police when the scandal broke, but when the case came to trial, Euston simply denied everything in court and assumed, correctly as it turned out, that his word would be believed against that of a 'common boy'. Euston was acquitted.

Even more aristocratic and well connected than Euston was

Mr Brown, who was, in reality, Lord Arthur Somerset, equerry to and personal friend of the Prince of Wales. He was the unluckiest of all the aristocrats associated with Cleveland Street, but as we will see he still evaded the prosecution that befell the smaller fish.

It was in 1889 that the tottering edifice built up at 19 Cleveland Street came tumbling down and when it came down rumours immediately began to circulate that a member of the royal family was involved.

The discreet aura surrounding 19 Cleveland Street was shattered because a curious tradition had developed among telegraph boys employed by the Post Office. Aged twelve and upwards, these young men dashed around the city delivering telegrams – at that time the only rapid form of communication – but they were badly paid and, on the grapevine, it had become well known that they could supplement their earnings by working as rent boys.

A number were employed at Cleveland Street and if the work was risky it was not because the boys might be caught there but rather because they might be caught by their Post Office employers with more money than they could possibly have earned legitimately. A boy called Charles Swinscow was discovered to have more than fourteen shillings in his pocket – far more than he would earn in a month as a telegraph boy. The police were called and he admitted he had earned the extra money at Cleveland Street. As Glenn Chandler, the biographer of Jack Saul, records, 'There was a boy prostitution racket going on at the General Post Office at St Martin Le Grand.'

Swinscow was questioned at length by the police and his information led to the arrest of several other boys, which led, in turn, to a warrant for the arrest of Hammond. But when the police arrived at Cleveland Street, the house had been locked up and Hammond was already gone. With his network of loyal aristocratic customers, he had been warned and he escaped, via his brother's house at Gravesend, to France. He was never to return to England.

The story of Cleveland Street and rumours about royal involvement quickly reached the ears of servants at Buckingham Palace and at the Prince of Wales's London home, Marlborough House, as Agnes Cook recalled:

My mum and my aunts knew people who worked below stairs at both Buckingham Palace and Marlborough House. It might have just been them hearing rumours and spinning a bigger story out of them, but everyone believed that the Prince of Wales's son Eddy was involved in that Cleveland Street business. The servants thought of Eddy as what they used to call a Nancy boy – that meant he looked and sounded and behaved in a very effeminate way. There were always jokes about him marrying a nice young man or people would ask if it took him long to get into his stays.

Cleveland Street historian Glenn Chandler explains that as the investigation into the scandal gathered pace, a round-the-clock watch was kept on No. 19. Lord Arthur Somerset, one of

Hammond's most enthusiastic customers, was spotted trying to enter the house not once but several times. He was clearly not yet aware that Hammond had made a run for it.

Word that his son might be prosecuted eventually reached Somerset's father, the Duke of Beaufort, who was rumoured to be an enthusiastic seducer of under-age girls. Beaufort was determined to extricate his son from the impending scandal.

Then, with the rumour mill working overtime, the police investigation suddenly stopped. Senior figures in the government were so horrified by what might be about to happen that they instructed the police to halt the investigation. Both the director of public prosecutions and Prime Minister Lord Salisbury insisted there should be no attempt to bring Hammond back to the UK and that the police should treat the case as a minor and purely local affair – it was hoped that this would ensure a minimum of publicity.

Prime Minister Salisbury insisted on playing a waiting game – he was determined to allow just enough time for Lord Arthur Somerset to escape abroad. And that's exactly what happened. Somerset's father secretly sent money to others who might give evidence against his son to make sure they stayed out of England.

In the end, only the boys involved were prosecuted. When they were brought to trial, the presiding magistrate had been told in no uncertain terms that he must not mention anyone other than those before him.

And this is where Prince Albert Victor enters the picture.

Some say that Eddy, who was notoriously unmanly by the standards of the time, was implicated in the Cleveland Street scandal only because Lord Somerset's solicitor, Arthur Newton, cunningly mentioned his name to ensure that Somerset was allowed to escape. The logic was that if Somerset were brought to trial, the names of other even more prominent men might come out and Newton knew the government would do anything to prevent that from happening. If this is true then Newton, the solicitor involved, was certainly doing his utmost for his client, but it is difficult to believe that he would risk his reputation and future employment to protect just one client. After all, Newton was part of the establishment and it was going to be very difficult for him to ensure that he would not become known as the source of a rumour highly damaging to Prince Eddy and the whole of the royal family. Newton was certainly very well paid by the Duke of Beaufort and it may well be that he was deliberately paid enough to cover the risk to his future employment of implicating a prince.

Money, then as now, talks and it is undoubtedly true that everyone was prepared to lie to get off the hook. Lord Euston, who was too deeply implicated to avoid a court appearance, certainly fabricated a story that would enable him to escape prosecution without the need to spend the rest of his life abroad. Euston claimed that he had been approached in the street by a young man who had offered him a card and suggested he might like to accompany him to what today we would probably call a striptease. Illegal at the time, of course, but not at all in the same

league as visiting a male brothel. Euston, standing in the witness box, explained that having discovered there were no naked
women at Cleveland Street, he immediately left. Just like the
Prince of Wales in his various court appearances, Euston was
considered too important to be cross-examined and the fact that
at least one of the boys involved had identified Euston accurate-
ly was ignored. Euston's story was accepted and he left the court
a free man, although today it is generally agreed his story about
going to Cleveland Street to see naked women rather than men
was certainly a lie.

Eye-witness evidence against Somerset and the fact that he
had also been caught twice trying to enter Cleveland Street
could not so easily be circumvented. For the government and
the Prince of Wales, this opened up the prospect of a terrifying
scandal – too much was at risk, which was why the investigation
had been halted. It allowed just enough time for Somerset to
leave the country.

Rumours that Prince Eddy was a regular visitor to Cleveland
Street have persisted to this day. There is no hard evidence either
way – none of the boys who worked at Cleveland Street identified him directly, but since the boys were not believed anyway
(when it came to allegations against Euston, for example), that
is hardly proof that Eddy was never at Cleveland Street. And it
is highly likely that any statement that implicated him would
not have been recorded by the police. If the Prince of Wales's
equerry could not be prosecuted, it hardly seems likely that
his son would be allowed to appear in the dock charged with

a crime that, if it had led to his conviction, might well have destroyed the royal family.

It is curious, too, that Eddy should have been picked on as the royal who visited a male brothel. There were other royal men – most notably the notorious Prince of Wales himself – who might just as easily have been chosen if the plan was to involve a member of the royal family in order to stop the prosecution of others. Why did Newton pick Eddy?

If Agnes Cook is to be believed, it was widely accepted both in London society and among those who worked for the royal family that Eddy was somehow not like other men. Perhaps Somerset's solicitor hinted at Eddy's involvement because everything about his character made his involvement seem plausible.

Of course, as we have seen with many royal scandals, conclusive evidence is hard to come by. But Somerset himself certainly hints at a cover-up in a letter he wrote to his friend Lord Esher: 'I have never mentioned ... [Eddy's] name except to Probyn, Montagu and Knollys when they were acting for me and I thought they ought to know. Had they been wise, hearing what I knew and therefore what others knew, they ought to have hushed the matter up.'

Beyond that, anything that might have emerged suggesting Eddy had been a Cleveland Street customer would have been ruthlessly suppressed. And if the rumours had no basis in fact, it is curious that the Lord Chief Justice was tasked with keeping a close eye on the court case on behalf of Eddy and that Treasury Solicitor Augustus Stephenson discussed Eddy's involvement in coded letters to other members of his department.

Eddy's biographers have reached widely differing views on the matter of his sexuality. In his 1976 account of Cleveland Street, H. Montgomery Hyde concludes that 'there is no evidence that he was homosexual, or even bisexual'. Theo Aronson, by contrast, in his 1994 book *Prince Eddy and the Homosexual Underworld*, concludes that Eddy was 'probably homosexual'.

Certainly, establishment efforts to control the trial, suppress the evidence and ensure that only the prostitutes were prosecuted have a whiff of cover-up about them. And always there is that nagging question – why would an establishment figure such as Somerset's solicitor Newton risk destroying his own career by implicating the second in line to the throne simply to get his own client, Eddy's father's equerry, off the hook?

It might be that Eddy was just unlucky. Certainly, he seemed to attract scandal wherever he went – he was said to be Jack the Ripper and it was claimed he was a regular at a transvestite club where he was known as Victoria. But whatever the truth of the extent of his involvement in these and other scandals, it is a fact that Eddy's name will be for ever linked with one of the most extraordinary scandals of the nineteenth century.

Eddy died in 1892 aged just twenty-eight from pneumonia. His parents were heartbroken and obituarists had nothing but praise for the dead prince, but his reputation has never really recovered from Cleveland Street and other scandals. Later biographers, including Philip Magnus in 1964, went so far as to say that Eddy's early death was 'an act of providence' that kept an unsuitable king from the throne and replaced him with his worthy (if rather dull) brother, George V.

But what happened to the boys who were brought to trial? On the principle (now largely discarded) that those who sold their bodies were always more reprehensible than those who bought them, the boys were found guilty but, curiously, they were given unusually lenient sentences. Again, the rumour mill began to turn and it was widely agreed that the light sentences were the result of pressure from a government desperate for the whole scandal to go away. Harsh sentences would have drawn the fire of the newspapers which might have pointed out the discrepancy between the treatment of the boys and the treatment of their clients.

And there is one final curious fact: after his death, all Prince Eddy's papers, all the documentation concerning his life and all his letters were immediately destroyed.

CHAPTER TWELVE

'NOT A WOMAN AT ALL'

'Hark the herald angels sing,
Mrs Simpson's pinched our king'
POPULAR SONG

Edward VII was followed by his son George V (1865–1936) who reacted to the wild and scandalous excesses of his father by becoming as dour and respectable as his grandmother Queen Victoria. But George V's eldest son, later Edward VIII (1894–1972), was far more like his pleasure-loving grandfather.

A vast amount has been written about the abdication of King Edward VIII. The king's relationship with Wallis Simpson (1896–1986) may well be the most discussed relationship in English history. We know a great deal about the scandal of the couple's sympathies with Hitler and Nazi Germany but perhaps less well known is the fact that, despite this being the great romance of the twentieth century, neither Wallis Simpson nor the Duke of Windsor were faithful to each other either before or during their marriage.

Born at a time when the British royal family could still expect almost universal deference, Edward as Prince of Wales was seen as a sort of prototype pop star. He had a charmingly self-deprecating air, he liked informality and he seemed to reject the stiff, cold, emotionless world of his father, King George V. He was a modern prince who liked dancing and clubbing, who enjoyed travel and the company of beautiful women. His apparent shyness and his wistful sideways glance are both remarkably reminiscent of a look perfected much later in the twentieth century by Diana, Princess of Wales.

Edward's hideaway, the place where he was most able to be himself, was Fort Belvedere, effectively a small palace in the grounds of Windsor Castle. Originally known as Shrubs Hill Tower, Fort Belvedere was built in the 1750s as a folly; it was deliberately situated at the top of Shrubs Hill to allow wide-ranging views across nearby Virginia Water and beyond. Largely rebuilt as a house in 1828, Fort Belvedere has always been lived in by members of the royal family, but none so scandalous as Edward, Prince of Wales.

At Fort Belvedere Edward behaved in a completely uninhibited way. Visitors were astonished at just how informal he could be. He would offer visitors a drink and then go and get it himself. Rather than restrict himself to the traditional royal pursuits of hunting, shooting and fishing, he enjoyed gardening, especially at Fort Belvedere, and he played golf, a game seen as dreadfully suburban in aristocratic circles. That attitude continued well into the 1960s when Labour politician Anthony Crosland said of the Prime Minister Harold Wilson, 'The bloody man plays golf.'

But a modern psychologist might have made a great deal of the darker side of Edward's nature. Growing up in his emotionally repressed family, Edward craved female company of a particular sort. He wanted women who would mother him, console him and reassure him, and in this he was, again, remarkably like his grandfather Edward VII who was always drawn to large maternal women. In more recent times we have seen faint echoes of this desire for a mother figure in Prince Charles's relationship with Camilla, Duchess of Cornwall. Charles and Camilla's relationship seems always to have had far more to do with Camilla's maternal strength rather than, say, her looks.

Charles has publicly stated that his childhood was unhappy partly because he was sent to a school he hated and partly because his parents, and especially his mother, were almost always absent. As a small child Charles was looked after primarily by nannies while his mother toured the world. In an interview with the present author, a close friend of Charles who did not want to be named said:

Charles has a craving for safe, enduring maternal affection; Camilla combines this with a rock-solid character that Charles entirely lacks. Like many upper-class little boys back in the 1950s, he was expected to tough it out on his own from his earliest years. Anything else was seen as unmanly, but Charles was unusually sensitive and just couldn't do it. If anyone needed maternal affection it was Charles. And it was this need that made Philip rather despise Charles. The irony is that if Elizabeth, his mother, had been there for him when he was a small child, he might well have turned into a much tougher, more resilient adult who would not have had to cling to Camilla at the expense of his marriage to Diana.

There is also something quite masculine about Camilla and a similar quality of masculinity was key to Wallis Simpson's appeal to Edward. In the case of Mrs Simpson, it was a masculine air that hid an extraordinarily scandalous secret: allegedly, Wallis Simpson was, biologically speaking and according to diarist James Pope-Hennessy, 'not a woman at all'; she had both male and female sex organs.

In the young Edward, or David as he was known when he was the Prince of Wales, the public saw only a dazzlingly attractive prince who was conscientious, apparently hard working and concerned about the welfare of his people. As Andrew Morton points out in *17 Carnations: The Windsors, The Nazis and The Cover-Up*, in the 1920s Edward visited some forty-five countries in an official capacity, travelling more than 150,000 miles – quite an undertaking in the days before air travel. This certainly looked like dedication and it was only years later that people realised that this compulsive travelling had little to do with hard work and was largely a desperate attempt to escape the constraints and boredom of his life in England – a life he hated. Fort Belvedere was the only royal residence in which Edward felt he could be himself, but the inevitable round of royal protocol meant he had to spend time at Buckingham Palace, St James's Palace and Windsor, places still governed by stultifying rules laid down by

Queen Victoria and maintained to a great extent by his mother, Queen Mary.

Edward enjoyed the adulation of the crowds and the inevitable attentions of young women wherever he went. Those 150,000 miles gave him the chance to sleep with an almost endless stream of other people's wives. Such was the allure of royalty in this, the last era of deference, that a number of men whom Edward met on his world tours seemed almost flattered that Edward wanted to sleep with their wives. Edward's embarrassing sexual escapades were widely covered in the American and world press but almost nothing was mentioned in Britain – newspaper barons such as Lord Northcliffe were so much a part of the establishment that they had no intention of allowing their editors to publish anything that might embarrass people they were desperate to be accepted by.

Edward's interest in work, the real work of a modern monarch – checking his red boxes, dealing with letters and government papers and other business – was actually minimal. In fact, Edward loathed it and he did it so badly that the government approached the royal household in a discreet attempt to get someone else to oversee the prince's paperwork. According to a former member of Edward's staff at Fort Belvedere:

[He] used to put off looking at his paperwork for as long as possible and on many occasions, he was so tired and drunk by the time he forced himself to look through his papers that he would fall asleep on a nearby sofa leaving documents strewn about everywhere. He didn't care either if the staff picked up the papers which is amazing when you think he was the only person supposed to see them.

But there had been signs of this from Edward's earliest days as a public figure. Throughout his time as the Prince of Wales he showed a marked dislike for any official business. He lost important documents, showed them to his girlfriends, especially, later on, Wallis Simpson, and was completely reckless in his attitude to punctuality and politeness. He would frequently turn up late for official engagements or not turn up at all.

Edward loathed the idea that one day he must be king because he hated the world represented by his father; a world of stuffy duty and overly serious posturing. He wanted to be loved; the pin-up poster boy who was adored by millions of young women across the world despised what he called 'princing'. He described himself as a figure of 'weak, powerless misery'. His only relief from this perception of himself was continual travel and an endless series of girlfriends, and they were always girlfriends of a particular type: he detested shy, self-deprecating English aristocratic girls, preferring wise-cracking, confident and often controlling or at least self-assured women. His mistresses were invariably already married – indeed, it was the fact of their being married that was part of the appeal.

The truth is that the shy, handsome prince who seemed to be interested in the plight of the poor and less fortunate was actually a selfish, immature man who cared only for his own pleasure and wilfully misunderstood his role. When he visited the poor of

Northumberland or Wales and insisted 'something must be done', other members of the royal family were horrified – here was the future king meddling in political matters in a manner they saw as dangerously revolutionary. It was typical, they thought, of his recklessness. But in the public's eyes this modern prince could do no wrong. They saw only his instinct for compassion. They could not see, as palace officials could, that this apparently altruistic prince was in fact deeply disturbed. Officials saw an immature man who hated doing any serious work at all. He was also greedy and selfish – something borne out by his behaviour after his abdication when he chose to live permanently in France, not because he particularly enjoyed being in France, but because France was the only country that offered him residency without the need to pay any taxes. Edward would have preferred to live in America but he was told that if he chose America, his income would be taxed. He was outraged. Throughout his adult life, first as the Prince of Wales and then for the short period during which he had been the king, taxpayers footed the bill. Edward's role, he felt, was to tour the country and dominions – a role he enjoyed because he loved attention and praise – but otherwise to simply do as he pleased. In this respect, his character harks back to his grandfather Edward VII, another lazy, self-indulgent man who was seen by *his* parents as a rebel against duty. The great fear was that the young Prince of Wales's behaviour would lead to a scandal that might threaten the very existence of the monarchy. And as history shows, these fears were well founded.

* * *

Edward's greatest love before Wallis Simpson was Lady Furness, who referred to Edward as 'my little man' and the joke in London society was that she was referring not just to his childish dependency on her.

Edward's interest in sex seems to have been a secondary consideration. Indeed, there is some suggestion that he was both undersexed and not entirely heterosexual. The writer Andrew Morton quotes Anne Seagrim, who was Edward's private secretary from 1950 to 1954, as confirming this. She described his uncertainty about his sexuality and his ability to be a heterosexual man. Curiously, Seagrim also insisted that he was inherently scared of women. Referring to an early biography of Edward by Frances Donaldson, Seagrim wrote: '[She] misses the essential point about his character – his fundamental uncertainty about his sexuality and his ability to be a heterosexual man. He was fundamentally afraid of women.' This would fit with the idea that Edward needed the comfort of women who were mother figures, but he also needed to feel in their power. He wanted women who would control him. He enjoyed the slight feeling of apprehension this caused – a feeling that echoed the constant feeling of apprehension he felt in the presence of his decidedly unmaternal mother, Queen Mary. The attraction of the 'strong mother' type also echoes Edward VII's obsession with similar women.

Daisy Wright, whose mother worked as a domestic at Edward VIII's house, Fort Belvedere, which was the scene of many of Edward's encounters with Mrs Simpson and earlier lovers, thought Edward was essentially a feminine character:

He was fastidious about his clothes in a way that seemed very unmasculine to us. He also seemed tiny – he was only five feet seven inches tall after all – and delicate, painfully thin. He spoke in a very precise way and seemed almost camp with his limp hand movements and sort of prissy gestures. When he was in love with someone, whether it was Lady Furness, Freda Dudley Ward or Mrs Simpson, he was rather like a devoted puppy – or so my mother used to say. He wasn't particularly witty or amusing but he liked women who were witty and amusing and most of all he liked women who were a bit sharp with him at times. He liked to be scolded occasionally, told off as if he had been a naughty boy.

He also had a thing for young men. He was never as nice to the female servants as he was to the young male servants – my mother thought it was because he didn't fancy any of the girls! One young man who came in and did various jobs – I suppose he'd be called a sort of odd job man today – was very good looking and Edward apparently used to make all sorts of excuses to be with him. My mother told me the servants used to say, 'God, he's drooling after Johnny today.' Being the future king, he did as he pleased and it never occurred to him, at least at that time, that the servants, who were mostly invisible to him, might be gossiping behind his back but I'm afraid they did. Servants always gossiped. According to my mother, it was the only thing that made the job bearable. But as I say, if he was swooning over Johnny as he often was it would never occur to him to be discreet or worry about what the servants saw him get up to. My mother said it was all very odd and he did it with other young men too – he seemed desperate for physical contact with motherly women and handsome young men.

The past fifty years have shown us as never before how dysfunctional the royal family really is. In earlier ages, and certainly during the decade up to Edward becoming king, the mystery and mystique of the royal family was carefully and to a large extent successfully maintained. The public was allowed to see only a close-knit family devoted to duty and to upholding Christian values. George V had carefully drawn a line between his reign and the shockingly immoral reign of his father. For Edward, the solid family values image was a sham. In his biography of Wallis, Michael Bloch explains that Edward told his private secretary Sir Godfrey Thomas he was so depressed that at times he felt he might go mad. Lord Mountbatten noted how moods of 'unbearable depression' overtook the young king during royal tours – on shipboard he would retreat to his cabin, sometimes for days at a time. Mountbatten described him as 'a lonely person, lonely and sad'.

Only Freda Dudley Ward and his other mistresses could lift his spirits. But he was a mass of contradictions: he wanted to be ordinary, but hated it if anyone was over-familiar or did not give him the deference he felt was his due. In this respect, he was remarkably like Princess Margaret who hated people who saw only the princess when they met her, but tore people off a strip if they failed to curtsey to her.

All of Edward VIII's problems stemmed from his childhood. His father, George V, was cold and unemotional. His mother,

Queen Mary, was equally severe. They gifted a dark, gloomy out-look to their son from which he spent his life trying to escape.

To the outside world, Edward was a man of immense charm – even his enemies agreed that there was something unaffected and endearing about his social manner. Indeed, one of the main reasons the royal family forced him out of the country after his abdication was that they were terrified his charm and huge popularity would overshadow the new king who stammered and was socially ill at ease.

But there were more serious, darker reasons for their attitude to the king who abdicated and these reasons had to do not just with his support for Hitler and the Nazi regime, but with his increasingly scandalous private life.

*　　*　　*

Antisemitism has arguably always been a fact of life in England, especially among the upper classes. Virginia Woolf was married to a Jew yet her letters often contain unpleasant, antisemitic re-marks; T. S. Eliot's poem 'Gerontion' includes the lines:

> My house is a decayed house,
> And the Jew squats on the window sill, the owner,
> Spawned in some estaminet of Antwerp,
> Blistered in Brussels, patched and peeled in London

And if we go back a generation to the reign of Edward VII, the same holds true. It was common knowledge that Edward VII allowed the Jewish financier Sir Ernest Cassel into society only in return for money and financial advice. Edward's aristocratic friends disliked inviting Cassel to various country houses, but if the king insisted, they had no choice. As Andrew Morton points out, Edward VIII was, 'like many of his class, instinctively anti-Semitic – Buckingham Palace did not employ Jews or Catholics in positions of any prominence in the Royal Household until well into Queen Elizabeth II's reign'.

Ingrained antisemitism among the intelligentsia and aristocracy made many sympathetic to Germany's increasingly unpleasant treatment of Jews. Many of Edward VIII's oldest friends – and indeed many of his relatives – were German and he was instinctively sympathetic to the German view of the world at that time. Many German aristocrats with links to the Nazis were his relatives. Edward spoke fluent German, which he'd learned as a child. Despite the Great War and the royal family's change of name from Saxe-Coburg to Windsor, the Germans were much closer to the British than any other European nation. The echoes we hear down the years from Victorian times were still audible – Victoria, after all, had always referred to 'dear, dear Germany'.

If we combine what we have seen of Edward's damaged childhood with his need always to be with controlling women and his instinctive sympathy towards Germany and German ideas about race, it is not difficult to see that his life was always likely to lurch towards disaster. Looking back from the 1950s, the royal courtier Alan 'Tommy' Lascelles, who knew Edward well, summarised his character:

[Edward] had, in my opinion and in my experience, no comprehension of the ordinary axioms of rational, or ethical, behaviour; fundamental ideas of duty, dignity and self-sacrifice had no meaning for him, and so isolated was he in the world of his own desires that I do not think he ever felt affection – absolute, objective affection – for any living being, not excluding the members of his own family.

The truth of Lascelles's analysis can perhaps best be seen when Edward became obsessed with Wallis Simpson, whose main role seems to have been not to have sex with Edward but to keep him amused and distracted. While she made him laugh and engaged his thoughts, she kept his depression at bay. And for all his charm, Edward could be ruthless.

In *After the Victorians*, A. N. Wilson describes what happened when Edward had tired of Mrs Dudley Ward:

Sometime in May 1934 the prince's mistress, Mrs Dudley Ward, was distracted by the illness of a daughter and remained out of touch with him [the prince] for some weeks. When she rang the switchboard at St James's Palace, she spoke to the telephonist whose voice she had heard on an almost daily basis for many years. 'I have something so terrible to tell you,' said the young woman, her voice trembling with emotion, 'that I don't know how to say it. I have orders not to put you through.' And that was that.

* * *

SCANDALS OF THE ROYAL PALACES

Many of Edward's biographers have noted his curious lack of masculinity as we have seen, but there was also something extraordinary about Wallis Simpson, as Daisy Wright recalled in a story told to her by her mother:

My mother liked the prince because he was courteous to her on the few occasions he noticed her – royalty paid no attention to servants in those days. But she wasn't so keen on Mrs Simpson so she may have been biased but this is what she told me. 'If the prince was odd and oddly feminine then what was much stranger was Mrs Simpson. She was gruff-voiced and much more masculine than the prince – all the servants noticed it but of course it was none of our business and you could be sacked for gossiping back then. It was only years later that anyone could talk about that sort of thing – as Prince of Wales and then king he could have had two heads and no one would have said anything against him. Later on, of course, we were no longer so in awe of the royals and more scandalous stories could be told. But we all commented on the fact that Mrs Simpson and the prince though clearly devoted to each other were curiously more like brother and sister than like lovers.

'I think the prince did like sex because when he slept with other women, they were often quite noisy but this didn't happen so much with Mrs Simpson. I think their relationship so far as we servants saw it was about looking after the prince. He slept with other women even after Mrs Simpson came along – sex with Mrs Simpson was not so important to him. He just wanted her to be the mum and dad he never really had.

'I only saw his father once but he was as stiff as a board – unsmiling, harsh, like a cardboard cut-out of a man. And his mother – goodness what an old stick she was! His parents were only interested in duty, duty, duty and the prince hated duty, but then his parents must have been horrified after the First World War that the royal family might have been kicked out as so many European kings and queens were kicked out, especially as they had so many close German relatives. Being whiter than white and serious about everything was, I suppose, their way of showing the British people that they were worth keeping on. But Mrs Simpson was a mystery to the staff. Like the prince she was very thin but she was also almost hyperactive and often aggressive – her quips and jokes were nasty sometimes and she used to say things in front of others that were cruel and humiliating – cruel to the prince I mean. She picked up a phrase used by Mrs Dudley Ward for example – she used to call the prince her little man and I think she used the phrase partly to have a dig at the prince about his earlier love but also, I'm sorry to say, it was a joke about his small stature and his small manhood if you get my drift.'

Wallis Simpson's curious air of masculinity has been the subject of some speculation, with her biographer Michael Bloch, who actually knew Mrs Simpson in her later years, suggesting that Wallis was probably intersex.

This theory or something like it was backed up by evidence gathered by Anne Sebba for her book *That Woman: The Life of Wallis Simpson, Duchess of Windsor*.

Sebba's argument is that Wallis Simpson was born with

ambiguous sex organs. Had she been born in the 1960s, her parents might have opted for 'normalising' surgery, either male or female; today she might have been given the chance to choose whether she wanted any medical intervention when she came of age. But when Wallis was born in the 1890s such treatment was unheard of and any sort of gender ambiguity would have been a source of shame and embarrassment, something to be hidden at all costs.

As Sebba puts it: 'There is now evidence to indicate ... she may have been born with what's currently called a Disorder of Sexual Development (DSD) or intersexuality, a term which embraces a wide range of conditions ... [which affects] approximately 4,000 [babies] in the UK [annually].'

It is certainly true that contemporaries commented on Wallis's deep, rasping voice. She also had large hands and her face had the angular hardness associated with male hormones. Biographer Michael Bloch has argued that she suffered from androgen insensitivity syndrome (AIS), a condition in which a child with XY chromosomes develops into a woman because their body does not respond to the large amounts of testosterone males produce early in life and during puberty. But the testosterone still produces some masculine features, including powerful muscles, large hands and a low-pitched voice – all of these were noted in Wallis by her contemporaries. Wallis may have compensated for her awareness of her masculinity by becoming determinedly sexual. This would certainly explain her eager pursuit of lovers both before and after her marriage to Edward. It would also explain, of course, those rumours about her extraordinary talents in the bedroom. This is something Daisy Wright hints at in her account of family memories about Wallis:

> My mother said everyone knew that Wallis was the man in the relationship – she made the jokes to Edward about how they must have an early night – and then she would wink at him. She was much more obviously physical with him and liked innuendoes. He was very confident with everyone – as you would expect of the Prince of Wales – but not with women. They threw themselves at him which made it easy for him but he liked women who took what was seen as the male role back then – by that I mean they chased him rather than the other way round.
>
> According to Mum, she used to drag him off to bed in the middle of the afternoon and though he loved this in many ways because it was so against all the boring convention he had grown up with – he sometimes looked almost afraid or he would say, 'Let's have another drink darling' or 'Let me finish my cigarette darling.'

Research suggests that as many as 10 per cent of marriages are never consummated and there is a strong possibility – extraordinary though it may seem – that this was the case with Edward and Mrs Simpson. According to biographer Anne Sebba, Wallis confessed to a friend that neither of her first two marriages had been consummated. In other words, Wallis's eagerness for the bedroom may well have had to do with sex, but perhaps not conventional penetrative sex, despite the claims that Wallis was a master of what was known as the Shanghai grip, a sexual technique claimed to make 'a match-stick feel like a cigar'!

Clearly the combination of Freda Dudley Ward's jibe about Edward's small penis and her claim that he was prone to premature ejaculation – details discussed by both Wallis's and Edward's biographers – at the very least suggests that Edward's sex life before he met Wallis was troubled. Meeting someone whose sex life was equally fraught might have been enormously appealing and it would have allowed both Edward and Wallis to get what they wanted sexually from the partnership. Regardless of whether Wallis suffered from AIS or another form of intersexuality, she seems to have been unable to have children.

And although Edward had a string of mistresses before his marriage, there is no hint that any of these amours led to unwanted pregnancies – or at least that has always been the conventional view. Daisy Wright has a different story:

According to my mother there were all sorts of rumours about Edward, from the completely mad – that he allowed men to have sex with Wallis while he watched for example – to the completely plausible. Anyway, one of her stories was as follows: 'A very pretty maid worked at Windsor for a few months a while before Edward met Mrs Simpson. She was confident and cheeky too and we knew Edward had taken a shine to her because though he hardly noticed most of us, she was treated to jokes and teasing. There was a certain look he liked, combined with a certain attitude and both the gardener's boy and the maid had this. Despite being a favourite with the prince, the maid vanished after about six months. Domestic staff always talked to each other and if someone was leaving for another position, we all knew about it. We all talked about it. But this pretty maid just disappeared. One day she was there, the next she was gone. We all wondered if Edward had made her pregnant – that was the usual reason for such a sudden departure. The girl would be paid off and given a generous allowance to try to stop word getting out. We didn't have any proof but her going was certainly very odd. And, of course, we all wanted to believe every bit of scandal as it was exciting – it brightened up our lives.'

What adds to the scandal is the fact that Wallis and Edward appear to have had an unwritten agreement that they would sleep with other people despite their passion for each other.

Daisy Wright again:

My mother always insisted that people would have been deeply shocked if they'd realised how promiscuous Edward and Mrs Simpson were. She said the servants referred to them as the bed-hoppers. Didn't matter where they were – Windsor Castle or Fort Belvedere – they always knew someone who would join in their games. My mother always said the servants didn't bat an eyelid – they just changed the sheets!

According to Daisy Wright, Edward's bed-hopping also happened at Balmoral, St James's Palace and even Sandringham. 'But he always took the greatest risks at Fort Belvedere where the long shadow of his father barely reached him.'

The appeal of a sexually ambiguous partner for someone who was himself sexually ambiguous – small, thin, slightly effeminate and certainly camp – is obvious and it may also explain Daisy Wright's insistence that, at least according to her mother, Edward was attracted to men as well as women:

> My mother used to say that it has always been no holds barred for royalty. If Edward fancied the gardener's boy, the gardener's boy would be too in awe to say no; if the Prince of Wales pulled the maid into bed, she would never mention it to anyone, would she? Who would believe a gardener's boy or a maid if they complained about a king in waiting? No one would believe them so they would just have to put up with it or leave, and leaving a good position in the home of the Prince of Wales might mean you'd never get another job. I mean you would never get a reference and in those days no reference meant no job.
>
> The rewards for having sex with Edward – or just going to bed with him – were potentially huge. It was a way to get the sort of money a servant could hardly earn in a lifetime.

It certainly seems likely that Wallis was trying to compensate for what she feared might be seen as her overly masculine nature by being 'boy mad' – a typical response to a disorder of sexual development or intersexuality.

Other hints are strongly suggestive of Wallis's curious intersexuality, including Daisy Wright's family memories:

> My mother insisted Mrs Simpson was like a man in every way. Flat as the proverbial ironing board and until a new maid got used to Mrs S's voice, the maid would insist there were two men

in the drawing room where in fact it was Wallis and Edward. Her voice was so deep. She was also the least maternal woman it is possible to imagine.

For Edward's part, his obsession with Wallis even led to rumours, almost certainly put about by palace officials, that he had inherited the Hanoverian strain of madness that afflicted his ancestor George III. Archbishop of Canterbury Cosmo Gordon Lang wrote to the then editor of *The Times* Geoffrey Dawson to say:

My dear Dawson, I have heard from a trustworthy source that His Majesty is mentally ill and that his obsession is due not to mere obstinacy but to a deranged mind.

More than once in the past he's shown symptoms of persecution-mania. This, even apart from the present matter, would lead almost inevitably to recurring quarrels with his ministers if he remained on the throne.

Lang was notoriously conservative and actively disliked the prince but even allowing for that, his judgement was based on what many agreed was an unbalanced passion. Like so many people at the time and afterwards, the establishment and the church simply couldn't understand how a woman of 'no breeding, little intelligence, and very little in the way of beauty' could make a king give up his throne.

Lang of course had reckoned without the pull of that ambiguous sexuality, that unrestrained libido, that combined masculine aggression with female sensibility.

Such things were not understood at the time and barely acknowledged.

* * *

Rather like his ancestor Edward II, Edward VIII was a man with little insight and almost no political interest at all. As well as being lazy, he was impetuous; when he was told he couldn't marry Wallis, he abdicated without first making sure that the details of what he would do after the abdication were settled. It was this lack of an agreed role that was to cause endless scandal in the years that followed.

Having abdicated in 1936, he quickly found that his family turned against him, largely it seems because his brother's wife – later the Queen Mother – could never forgive him for abandoning his duty and leaving his brother, who was ill-equipped to become king, to shoulder a responsibility that was never meant to be his. It was the beginning of a feud that was to last decades. Indeed, it would remain unresolved until Edward's death in 1972.

In exile, Edward became increasingly angry that not only did his brother, the new king, largely reject all requests for some kind of public role but he also refused to receive Wallis Simpson. The family and the British government also agreed that Wallis should never be allowed the appellation HRH. Worse still, the royal family and the British government made it clear that it would be better for everyone if Edward simply disappeared into obscurity. Even Edward's former friend and ally Winston Churchill thought this the wisest course. It was only when it was too late that Edward realised he should have agreed – formally agreed – before the abdication that he should have some public role.

We all know the famous story of King Lear. Like Lear, Edward gave his kingdom away and then felt he could still command the respect, power and attention he had enjoyed as king. For if there is one great truth about Edward it is that, as Tommy Lascelles hinted, he was too self-obsessed, perhaps even too stupid, to understand that however much he might have hated 'princing', he would hate his life far more when he had no 'princing' to do.

Feeling ostracised and undervalued, he and Wallis wandered aimlessly around Europe after they married in June 1937.

As Andrew Morton points out in *17 Carnations*, Edward so hated his sudden irrelevance that, aware of the increasing tensions between Germany and Britain, he began to see himself as the great peacemaker between the two countries. Instinctively seeing an opportunity, Hitler thought the disaffected and unhappy duke might be installed in a defeated Britain as Marshal Pétain was later installed in a defeated France.

British fears about the duke's Nazi sympathies increased dramatically when, soon after the abdication, the Duke and Duchess of Windsor, as they now were, embarked on a widely publicised tour of Germany, meeting Hitler and publicly expressing their admiration for the German leader.

Both Edward and Mrs Simpson had been sympathetic to the Nazi Party throughout the 1930s. Even allowing for the general feeling among the British upper classes that communism was by far the greatest threat, and that national socialism was a bulwark against left-wing revolution, the relationship between Edward VIII and Hitler is still extraordinary. That it existed and flourished throughout the 1930s is bad enough, but that it continued into and through the war is something the British public have struggled to forgive.

Despite his lack of intellect and his inability to see much beyond his own desires, the duke was not a naive player in all this. In fact, it is easy to see that in consorting with the Nazi regime, to the great embarrassment of the royal family and the British government, Edward was to some extent getting his revenge. He believed that he should have been given a significant public role, perhaps advising his brother and even the government. He thought his exclusion was vindictive and stupid and the fault of particular individuals within the royal family. What he refused to see was that his family wanted him out of the picture because they worried he would overshadow the new king. Edward was still hugely popular in England. Where Edward had been seen as charming and approachable, his brother, now George VI, seemed reserved and uncomfortable in public. And if the family had concerns so too did the government. It did not want a man who had shown such a total lack of interest in the workings of government when he was king to be meddling in politics or international affairs when he was no longer king. The government's view of the duke's abilities and attitudes was perhaps best summed up by the Earl of Crawford who thought Edward was 'too irresponsible a chatterbox to be entrusted with confidential information'.

And criticism of the duke's and duchess's behaviour was not confined to members of the British government and the royal family. Disturbed by what he saw as the duke's increasingly scandalous behaviour, his friend Major Edward Dudley Metcalfe (known to his friends as 'Fruity') wrote that the duke and duchess were behaving like 'two spoilt children'. Edward, on the other hand, completely rejected the idea that his new, lower status as an ex-king meant he should not interfere in politics; he felt that his role was to do far more than advise, encourage and warn. He desperately wanted peace between England and Germany and did not see that Hitler was simply using him to stop Britain intervening in his quest for world dominance.

Even when war began in 1939, Edward simply didn't understand the real issues or the seriousness of the threat; while Britain was in danger of invasion in 1941, for example, Edward wrote to Hitler asking if he would ensure that the duke's two houses, one in France and the other in Italy, would be left undamaged and not be looted. Hitler duly obliged.

But perhaps the most interesting glimpse into the Windsors' fantasy world came when, after the invasion of France, they left for Spain. Soon after arriving in Spain, Wallis realised she'd forgotten her favourite swimming costume so she and the duke negotiated safe passage for a servant to return all the way to Paris to retrieve it.

In June 1940 when Edward wanted to return to the UK, he telephoned Major-General Edward Spears, liaison officer between the French and British forces, to ask for a warship to be sent specially to Nice just to pick him up. Throughout the war, the Windsors behaved as if the whole thing was a slight mis-understanding and that whatever else was going on, their needs should come first.

Minister for Coordination of Defence Lord Caldecote con-firmed the British military's total distrust of the duke's motives: 'The activities of the Duke of Windsor,' he wrote, 'have been causing his majesty and myself grave uneasiness as his in-clinations are known to be pro-Nazi'. This was no more than the truth, but it wasn't just the natural inclination of a man who spoke German and was related to many members of the German aristocracy. It was also the reaction of a man who felt he had been badly treated by his home country. In truth, he wanted a role that was on a par, in terms of its importance and influence, with the role he had so rejected. Anything less was simply not good enough – which is why, when he was offered a job as deputy regional commissioner for Wales, he rejected it out of hand.

Even after the war – when Edward met his brother the king in 1945 after his shocking dalliance with the Nazis was known to his family if not to the public – he never gave up lobbying to be offered a suitably elevated post. He never succeeded. George VI insisted Edward could not work for the royal family in any capacity and could not live in England. As ever, the family ab-solutely refused to see Wallis or to accord her the appellation HRH. Edward, for so many years used to simply taking what-ever he wanted, was now trapped in a world in which he had no power, no influence at all.

Eventually so desperate were the British establishment to

remove this embarrassment – this dangerous embarrassment – from Britain that the duke was made Governor of the Bahamas. Even that job was sneered at by Edward and Wallis. They knew the point of the job was simply to get them as far as possible from Britain.

Edward's wartime fantasy that Hitler would invade Britain and put him back on the throne with Wallis at his side was dead. It had almost certainly been part of Hitler's plan and it appealed because Edward believed Britain would be defeated and he believed that Hitler would allow Wallis to reign by his side.

Looking back, the Windsors' flirtation with the Nazis was seen by many as just one more scandalous episode in the lives of a couple who were always drawn to outrageous behaviour. As early as 1936, for example, rumours had swirled through London high society that Wallis Simpson was not only sleeping with the Prince of Wales and her husband Ernest Simpson; she was also sleeping with the Nazi ambassador to Britain, Joachim von Ribbentrop. The rumours were confirmed when, in 1941, while Britain was suffering the massive deprivations of war, Wallis and Edward reached Florida on their way to their posting in the Bahamas.

The FBI was worried about the arrival of these known Nazi sympathisers. It was worried because, as part of a long investigation into those suspected of having links with the Nazis, it had interviewed a Benedictine monk called Father Odo. Odo was actually the Duke of Württemberg, a German aristocrat with close connections to the British royal family. Odo told investigators that in 1936 Ambassador von Ribbentrop had been Wallis

Simpson's lover and had given her seventeen carnations – one for every time they had slept together. She had also been sleeping at this time with Guy Trundle, a good-looking car salesman who was said to be as sexually voracious as Edward was sexually timid.

Odo insisted that Edward did not mind who Wallis slept with or how often, a view which coincides with Daisy Wright's mother's memoirs:

> I can remember my mother telling me that before they were married during those endless weekends at Fort Belvedere, Mrs Simpson and the Prince of Wales would have little parties that ended with people disappearing into various bedrooms and not always with their wives and husbands. She used to laugh because the servants were more upset by the fact that they seemed to be going to bed in the middle of the afternoon which meant we would have to tidy and clean twice that day!

Doing as he pleased came naturally to Edward so when a small publisher issued a book that mentioned in passing that the duke and Mrs Simpson had slept together before their marriage, the duke threatened to sue on the grounds that the story was untrue and the publisher had to pay crippling damages. But the duke knew that the story *was* true. Like his grandfather Edward VII, he was quite happy to lie to protect his own and his wife's reputation and had the case reached court, there is no doubt he would have happily committed perjury.

According to Daisy Wright's family memories, her mother was 'amazed when she heard the prince denying he'd slept with Mrs Simpson because when they were together in those early days, they hardly did anything else except sleep together!'

More shockingly, Daisy Wright recalls that:

Mrs Simpson slept with other people far more often than the prince did. Sometimes the prince would wander in the garden while Mrs Simpson had sex with a visitor and sometimes the prince would join them in the bedroom. I'm not sure he actually jumped in to bed with Mrs Simpson and whoever else it happened to be but he was certainly in the room. My mum said the servants were more and more amazed because they grew up thinking people behaved themselves! They would have been ashamed to be part of the sort of carrying on that went on at Fort Belvedere.

And if Daisy Wright's mother thought little of Edward and Mrs Simpson's morals, she was even less impressed at how an immensely rich man could behave as if he didn't have 'two pennies to rub together':

My mother insisted that Edward hated to spend his own money – he hated paying his servants, his tailor, the tradesmen, everyone – well, everyone that is except Mrs Simpson! He always checked that any invitation wouldn't involve him in any expense and my mother said that when he went to live abroad this got much worse.

Daisy Wright's family memories include not just Edward and Mrs Simpson's unconventional love life and their attitude to money. Her mother also recalled that the couple drank a great deal and even experimented with drugs:

> Many people knew that Edward's favourite brother George, Duke of Kent, was a notorious drug user. According to my mother, very few people outside their immediate circle knew that Edward and Wallis also took drugs at Fort Belvedere. Like his brother, Edward loved cocaine. Mind you, taking cocaine in the 1930s was not such a shocking thing as it may sound because at that time and until well into the 1950s, you could find cocaine in almost every medicine on sale in Boots! It was easy for Edward and his brother and their friends to get as much cocaine as they liked because it was not illegal.

According to Daisy, it was rumoured that Edward and Mrs Simpson loved cocaine because it helped Edward sexually. 'You have to remember that before the abdication Edward's life was all about his pleasure – even on his world tours his main concern was always to get women into bed and he saw cocaine as a bit of an aphrodisiac.'

Edward's pursuit of women is confirmed by socialite Diana Cooper who summed up his life as a young man when she said he was 'never out of a woman's legs'.

Much of Edward's outrageous behaviour was the result of his hatred of what he saw as the sheer, stultifying boredom of being a royal prince. He was also, of course, reacting against the dull conservatism of his own family, a conservatism that was almost always harsh and snobbish in its judgements. And it is certainly true that his family's reaction to Wallis was at times almost vicious – she was described by various senior members of his family as 'a witch', 'common' and a 'gold digger'. But the more they hated her, the more Edward insisted he would not give her up.

* * *

Perhaps the greatest scandal surrounding Edward and Mrs Simpson has yet to be fully uncovered. It began in 1945 when George VI sent the art historian Anthony Blunt on a secret mission to Germany. Blunt went on to haunt the corridors of Buckingham Palace as surveyor of the queen's pictures under Elizabeth II while simultaneously working as a Soviet spy. At the time of his mission to Germany, his spying activities were unknown. Indeed, he was considered a pillar of the establishment. Ostensibly his mission was to obtain letters written between the Empress Vicky, one of Queen Victoria's daughters, and Frederick III of Prussia during the latter part of the nineteenth century. But letters written so long ago hardly seemed to justify the cloak of secrecy that covered and still covers Blunt's journey to Germany.

The letters were held at Schloss Friedrichshof. There were also diaries in the dusty boxes in which the correspondence had languished for more than half a century. Various accounts exist of what happened when Blunt reached the castle but it seems likely that the papers Blunt was really after were not Vicky's at all. They were highly incriminating letters from the Duke and Duchess of Windsor to Hitler and other prominent Nazis. Some reports say the letters were removed quickly and un-checked by Blunt; other reports suggest Blunt made a microfilm of the incriminating letters, but only after American officials had resisted requests for access until the castle library had been checked and supposedly tidied up by them. The Americans were in charge as the castle was under their jurisdiction in the imme-diate post-war period.

Whatever the precise details, we know that a large quanti-ty of correspondence was moved with American agreement to Windsor, where it remains under lock and key to this day. His-torians have been quick to seize on the rich irony that a traitor was sent to see if he could secure letters that might otherwise expose an ex-king as a traitor. It seems certain that many of the letters and telegrams from the Windsors were deeply and em-barrassingly incriminating, but the problem was what to do with them. As Andrew Morton points out in *17 Carnations*, the royals were adept at destroying any written correspondence that might be embarrassing – Edward VII, for example, destroyed much of his mother's correspondence – but for some reason this was felt unwise with the Schloss letters. After the irony of Blunt being sent to collect the letters there was to be a further richly ironic episode when royal courtier Alan 'Tommy' Lascelles asked MI5 head Guy Liddell for advice on what to do with the re-trieved letters. Liddell, like Blunt, was a double agent and while heading up the British secret service he too was working for the KGB.

The most incriminating material in the Windsor file, as the cache of letters came to be known, is a series of telegrams sent by senior Nazis to senior Fascists in Spain at the time the duke and duchess were living in Spain. The telegrams suggest an astonishing level of complicity between the Windsors and Britain's enemies. In fact, the letters and telegrams were considered so damaging that British officials pressed the Americans to destroy their copies of the material, but the Americans refused for reasons that have never been made clear. It appears the Spanish and Germans had discussed the fact that they felt the duke could easily be persuaded to head up a puppet government in the UK in the event of Britain's defeat by the Nazis. It was the fact that the telegrams express their certainty that a bitter and angry former king would be delighted to supplant his brother that had to be suppressed.

The difference of viewpoint between the Americans and the British was neatly summed up in a top-secret memo written by United States state department director of European affairs John Hickerson and quoted by Andrew Morton:

I am convinced the British government will adamantly resist any suggestion on our part that any of the documents relating to the Duke of Windsor be made public. There is throughout the United Kingdom an unreasoning devotion to the monarchical principle and an almost fanatical disposition to do everything possible to protect the good name of the institution of the monarchy.

In a sense the whole history of the monarchy in Britain has been about protecting the institution of the monarchy in the face of the scandalous behaviour of individual monarchs, whether those monarchs were seen as incompetent and perverse, like Edward II, or unscrupulous, greedy and lecherous like so many monarchs from James I on. But the desire for personal fulfilment, to control one's own personal life at the expense of royal duty, reaches a particularly low point in Edward VIII.

For many years after the end of the Second World War, a group of American and British historians tried to get access to the Windsor file. Eventually it was realised that the act of suppressing the file created far more damaging rumours about what it contained than were justified by the actual contents. This was confirmed when leaked material revealed that the Windsors had behaved badly but that their behaviour did not quite amount to treason. Of course, there were and still are those who believe that only those parts of the Windsor file that are the least damaging to the monarchy have ever been revealed and that the cache of papers includes material so harmful it will never be released.

The current view, but one based on that highly selective release of material, is that Edward was naive and foolish rather than deliberately treacherous. His weak point, as ever, was Wallis – the Fascists hinted that Wallis would be able to reign at Edward's side if he agreed to their proposals. This was hugely tempting for the ex-king as it would achieve what he had always hoped to accomplish and it would be sweet revenge on those who had forced him out.

Of course, opinions differ and the extent of Edward's genuine sympathy for Nazi Germany is very difficult to assess. It is certainly true that the Nazis' antisemitism struck a chord with Edward. Before the war, at his Fort Belvedere hideaway, Edward and Wallis and their friends – including Fascist leader Oswald Mosley – expressed views that were entirely supportive of Germany and Hitler and their policies toward the Jews at that time. Daisy Wright recalls her mother's insistence that Wallis and Edward 'absolutely loved all things German and they thought the Jews were grubby trouble makers who were only interested in making money'.

Along with most English aristocrats, Edward and Wallis saw Hitler as a man who had brought prosperity and stability to Germany, and his anti-Jewish acts seemed only excessive rather than murderous, especially to a man like Edward who was himself deeply antisemitic. In the 1950s the journalist Frank Giles overheard the duke blaming the war on 'Anthony Eden ... and Roosevelt and the Jews'. As Governor of the Bahamas, Edward had blamed civil unrest on 'men of Central European Jewish descent, who had secured jobs as a pretext for obtaining a deferment of [the] draft'.

Of course, the duke himself always insisted that it was in the interests of Spanish and German agents in 1940 to give their masters the impression that the duke was on the Axis powers' side, but then, as was said about another post-war scandal, involving Christine Keeler, he would say that, wouldn't he?

The truth is that Edward's right-wing views and support for Germany continued in private for the rest of his life. He refused to jettison his belief that Britain should have made peace with Germany even after the invasion of Poland in 1939. If, as the duke had predicted, Germany had defeated Britain in 1940–41, it is hard to believe he would have refused the role of head of state if it had been offered to him with the promise that Wallis should be made queen. It should be remembered that Edward never actually expressed a desire to abdicate. He wanted to be king, but on his own terms – that is, with Wallis Simpson as queen consort.

Edward's real attitude to the Nazis is perhaps best seen in a diary entry written by British diplomat Sir John Balfour after he had dinner with the duke and duchess in the late 1940s: 'Both of them seemed oblivious to Nazi misdeeds and were at one in thinking that, had Hitler been handled differently, war with Germany might have been avoided.'

Behind this refusal to condemn Hitler lies an idea that was common in the 1920s and 1930s: European aristocrats felt that however bad Fascism might be it was better than communism and at the time it seemed to many people that a choice had to be made between the two. The duke loathed communism because he felt it was out to destroy the worlds of royalty and aristocracy. After all, Russian communists had murdered his godfather Tsar Nicholas in 1917.

One of the greatest mysteries about Edward VIII is that he could easily have chosen to remain king and with Wallis at his side – as his mistress. But he insisted on marrying her. Why? His own behaviour as a young man had shown he cared nothing for the sanctity of marriage. Before Wallis, as we have seen, he had a string of married lovers and he was not bothered by the fact that their husbands were often his friends. Perhaps deep down, like the spoilt child he was, Edward wanted to marry Wallis because he had been told he could not; no one was going to tell him what to do or what not to do. He was king and he would rule his private life absolutely. The abdication on this reading was a kind of gigantic tantrum.

Giving Wallis the marriage she craved also satisfied Edward's need to abase himself in front of her. He was frequently seen by visitors to Fort Belvedere on his knees painting her toenails or jokingly allowing her to use his prone form as a footstool, and it was Edward who always rushed to get Wallis a drink, to check that she was not sitting in a draught, that she had everything she needed. Daisy Wright's mother recalled that Edward seemed to enjoy being subservient to Wallis. Giving up the throne for her satisfied a similar desire. It was the best gift Edward could give her; the ultimate sign that all he really wanted was to lie at her feet.

Early on in the relationship he had been able to shower Wallis with money and jewels, but having given her so much he searched constantly it seemed for something, anything he could give her that was greater than riches. Lady Diana Cooper confirms the extraordinary extent of the duke's generosity to Wallis: she recalled that at Christmas 1934 Edward had given Wallis the equivalent in 2021 values of £7 million, but this wasn't enough; it was more than enough for Wallis, but not enough for the king. He wanted, above all, to give Wallis a throne.

* * *

Protected by Churchill after the war and by the establishment's desire not to embarrass George VI and later Queen Elizabeth II, Edward became a nuisance they hoped would simply go away. Even in retirement in France his life was undignified. As we have seen, he chose to live there largely to avoid paying tax. And the tax issue was used to stop the duke living in England – the government could have waived any need for the duke and duchess to pay tax but refusing to do so was a convenient way to keep them out of the country.

* * *

In 1967 a plaque was unveiled in the Mall to Edward VIII's mother, Queen Mary. The royal family felt it was likely to cause less adverse press comment if they invited Edward and Wallis, however reluctantly, but the power of the scandal surrounding the abdication was still palpable, despite the passing of more than two decades. At the unveiling ceremony, the Queen Mother gave Wallis an unsmiling handshake. Wallis did not curtsey.

Even in death, there was no forgiveness. The duke died from cancer of the throat in 1972 and Wallis was invited to stay at

Buckingham Palace where she was photographed staring forlornly from an upper window. The duke was buried at Frogmore, Windsor, and when Wallis died in 1986 permission was granted for her to be buried next to her husband. Significantly, even in death, there was no real reconciliation – the duke and duchess's grave is set well apart from the graves of other, less troublesome monarchs.

CHAPTER THIRTEEN

RENT BOYS AT
CLARENCE HOUSE

'Between two evils, I always pick the one I never tried before.'

MAE WEST

Clarence House, a grand imposing building a few hundred yards along the Mall from Buckingham Palace, was described by the Queen Mother (1900–2002) as a 'horrid little house' when she was told it was to be her new home following the accession of her daughter Elizabeth II in 1952.

In fact, Clarence House is a palace in all but name. It was completed in 1827 for the Duke of Clarence, later William IV, one of the many sons of George III. The architect was John Nash, then at the height of his fame and known today primarily for the grand sweeping thoroughfare of Regent Street. Damaged during the Blitz, Clarence House's interior has been redesigned many times in response to changing fashions. The Queen Mother spent a fortune – several hundred thousand pounds – remodelling and renovating. As a result, very little of the original building remains.

But despite her dislike of the residence, the Queen Mother remained at Clarence House for the next half century and more. Throughout that time, her constant companion was her favourite servant and Page of the Backstairs William Tallon (1935–2007), a promiscuous, charming gay man who regularly brought back to Clarence House young men he had picked up in the clubs and bars of nearby Soho. Popularly known as 'Backstairs Billy', William is one of the most scandalous figures in royal history.

In conversations with the present author, William confessed that in his early days at Clarence House he was able to do almost as he pleased as there were no concerns about security at all:

> We were allowed to do whatever we liked and I was very proud of working at Clarence House so I would ask friends to come and see where I worked – they might come over in the evening and I would show them round. I would even give them a tour of the Queen Mother's private apartments – no one minded, least of all the Queen Mother.

As he grew in confidence and became a close friend of the Queen Mother, William's behaviour became increasingly outrageous – he would organise noisy drunken parties in his rooms, and he allowed a string of lovers to stay overnight. One or two of his favourite young men had been in and out of prison.

By the 1970s security had been tightened and officials complained that Billy's outrageous behaviour should be stopped. But the Queen Mother would not hear of it – she insisted that Billy should continue to come and go as he pleased. When the *News of the World* reported that a 'rent boy' had been invited back to Clarence House by Billy, she simply replied, 'Wasn't it kind of William to bring that young man in out of the rain.'

The suggestion that William should be reprimanded or even sacked was always met with the same response. The Queen Mother would say, even to her most senior officials, 'Your position is negotiable. William's is not.'

When told that William and other servants were gay – and bear in mind that homosexuality was illegal during much of this period – the Queen Mother replied, 'Well, without them we would have to go self-service, wouldn't we?' She also knew William's loyalties would never lose their focus on her, as he explained:

I was never going to have a family and I was absolutely devoted to the Queen Mother and she knew it. I was on call at Clarence House day and night, 365 days a year. The aristocratic advisers who worked for the Queen Mother absolutely hated the fact that she preferred my company because in those days – I'm talking about the 1960s and 1970s – it was perfectly acceptable to look down on a shopkeeper's son from the Midlands with no education, which is what I was. But what the Old Etonians and ex-Guards officers didn't realise is that people at the top – I mean aristocrats and the royal family – often get on better with people at the bottom like me. Aristocrats always feel they are nearly as good as the royals and they feel they can criticise. I never criticised.

William was famous for his tact, his good looks and his charm, which is why the Queen Mother so doted on him. They regularly went for tea together at the Ritz and would sit tête-à-tête, gossiping for hours. The Queen Mother especially enjoyed William's bitchy remarks about her friends and her courtiers, as William recalled:

> We were talking one day about a particularly pompous old land-owner who worked at Clarence House and I said to the Queen Mother, referring to this particular gentleman, 'Yes, she really loves herself, doesn't she?' For some reason, the Queen Mother thought this particularly funny and she laughed so much she almost choked. I think that was part of the thing she liked about me – most often her senior advisers were really dry old sticks, very serious and pompous. They assumed that protocol and etiquette were vital in their relations with the royal family but actually the Queen Mother and other royals hated all that formality because they had to put up with it all the time.

William certainly took the view that the Queen Mother's affection for him meant he could behave as scandalously as he liked. He had originally never dared to bring more than one young man into Clarence House, but as the years passed he grew more outrageous and even organised what he himself described as 'mini-orgies'.

Tommy Burns, who knew William well in the 1950s and 1960s, explains:

> William told me that everyone at Clarence House was gay – he meant everyone below stairs, as it were. He said it was absolutely

ideal for a gay man at the time. It wasn't well paid but you got to live in a beautiful house – William's rooms were actually rather lovely – it was glamorous and you were unlikely to get into trouble if the police stopped you for cruising. As soon as you told them where you worked, they usually let you go.

More interestingly, William also told me that he had worked at Buckingham Palace for a short while before moving with the Queen Mother to Clarence House and that he had been seduced by a fellow servant just weeks after starting work aged just fifteen!

William certainly loved the Queen Mother but he also loved being among so many young gay men – almost all the young male staff at Buckingham Palace, Kensington Palace and Clarence House were gay. As William used to say, the goings-on at night were mind-boggling. He invited me to one late-night party and we even dressed up in some of the Queen Mother's clothes – she loved all that soft floating pink material and so did William. At different times during the party, groups of us – in twos and threes – would go off and have sex in another room. William even had sex in one of the Queen Mother's rooms! It was all so exciting. I can't begin to tell you. You have to remember we were doing all this in a royal palace and at a time when it was still illegal. We were living dangerously, and it added to the excitement of the sex. We sometimes worried that if we were caught William would be sacked, but he didn't worry so in the end we didn't either.

Eventually William's outrageous behaviour led to a compromise between the senior advisers and the Queen Mother. She hated the idea of curtailing William's activities because they made him happy but worries about security were growing. The compromise was to give William one of the lodges at the Clarence House gate on to the Mall. Here he could party to his heart's content, and with anyone who took his fancy, but technically his young friends would not be in the same building as the Queen Mother and William would still be on call whenever the Queen Mother needed him.

For the senior Clarence House staff, William's reckless sex life, as they saw it, was only one of a number of problems. A far greater irritation was the Queen Mother's increasing infatuation with a man they thought entirely unsuitable.

The parallels with Queen Victoria and John Brown are remarkable. In Brown Victoria found a no-nonsense man who had none of the artificial airs and graces of the effete aristocrats with whom she was surrounded. Brown teased and cajoled, he scolded and reproved; he treated the queen as if she were an ordinary woman and she loved it.

William entranced the Queen Mother but not quite in the same way. There was no real physical attraction as there undoubtedly was between Victoria and Brown, but Tallon put aside all ceremony when he dined with the Queen Mother. He refused to conform to court etiquette, told her outrageous stories, mocked the stuffed shirts who despised him and, above all, made her laugh. Like Victoria, the Queen Mother had spent her life being intimate only with those who shared her aristocratic background; in Brown and Tallon the two women found men who were extremely ordinary and supremely themselves.

Tommy Burns remembered seeing the Queen Mother and William together:

There was a chemistry between them; no doubt at all about that. The Queen Mother told William that her life would be pointless and boring without him. She looked forward to seeing him each day and was irritable when she spent time in her other houses and he was not there. She absolutely doted on him because in truth they were like husband and wife, and that was a major scandal from the courtiers' point of view. William deliberately annoyed and taunted these men; he knew that he was making enemies and he said to me once, 'I'm going to be in terrible trouble when the Queen Mother dies. They are going to crucify me.'

And he was right.

It is ironic that the greatest scandal associated with William Tallon was not in the end his outrageous sexual behaviour at Clarence House; it was the way he was treated after the Queen Mother died in 2002. Within weeks of her death, William was evicted from Gate Lodge and sent packing to a tiny council flat in Kennington. The palace offered him no support and his insistence that the Queen Mother had promised he could remain in the Clarence House lodge for his lifetime fell on deaf ears. 'It is ironic that I came from Coventry and now I've been sent to Coventry!' he bitterly quipped.

The disaster he had predicted had come to pass and after more than fifty years' royal service, William found life outside the palace almost unbearable. He began to drink heavily and was found dead in his flat just a few years later in 2007, aged seventy-two.

However, even in death there was more scandal to come.

According to one of William's Kennington neighbours, within days of his death something strange happened outside the flat:

> We knew William had worked for the Queen Mother because he was friendly with the neighbours and liked to boast about his former work. We kept an eye on the flat after he died and about a week later two expensive cars pulled up outside. Several very smartly dressed men got out and because they were vaguely important looking, we assumed it must be something to do with William. For the next hour or so they removed boxes and files from William's flat and piled them into the car. They drove off and never came back.

William's friends believe the royal family were terrified that he had left a diary and that it might fall into the wrong hands, as Tommy Burns explains:

> He was always talking about his diary – Billy's Black Book, he called it – and that it would cause a sensation and keep him in luxury when it was published after his retirement. I don't think he ever *would* have published anything, but he liked to tease the courtiers and make them think they were in it. They were so terrified I'm sure they organised a discreet raid on his flat to remove anything, including the diary, that might be embarrassing. It was a huge scandal that never reached the newspapers because whoever took the papers was just too good at covering their tracks.

CHAPTER FOURTEEN

LOVE AND LOSS: PRINCESS MARGARET, DIANA AND MEGHAN MARKLE

'Decency is indecency's conspiracy of silence.'

GEORGE BERNARD SHAW

After the Second World War, royal scandals seemed to come, as Shakespeare might have said, not as single spies, but in battalions. It was almost as if the old world of restraint, partially thrown off in the roaring 1920s and then finally killed off in the 1960s, had changed British society out of all recognition. Both the royal family and ordinary people began to question and even reject long-accepted values about duty, hard work, marriage and, especially, sexual morality.

The most famous post-war royal scandal – centred on Kensington Palace – was of course that created by the love affair between Princess Margaret (1930–2002) and Group Captain Peter Townsend (1914–95). This has been covered in great depth by numerous historians, not least in the present writer's book

Kensington Palace: An Intimate Memoir from Queen Mary to Meghan Markle.

Margaret wanted to be free to choose whom she would marry regardless of rules set out centuries earlier. Her wish to marry Peter, who was a decorated war hero, created an atmosphere of moral panic in the royal family for two reasons: first, he was a commoner and second, he was divorced. Divorce in the 1950s was still seen as disgraceful; it also went against the teachings of the church. Since Margaret's sister was queen and therefore head of the Church of England, this was a real problem.

The Royal Marriages Act of 1772, pushed through Parliament at the insistence of George III simply to keep control of his sons (who, as we may recall, had a tendency to marry Catholics), might easily have been revoked so that Queen Elizabeth II (1926–) could more easily have given permission for her sister's marriage to a divorced man, but the deeply conservative advisers who surrounded the Queen pressed her not to allow the marriage. Indeed, they also pressed her to remove Peter from the country – he was sent to Brussels – to prevent the marriage from taking place.

In a statement, Margaret insisted that in ultimately deciding not to marry Peter, she had chosen duty over personal happiness, but this was only part of the story. In fact, for the rest of her life, she remained bitter and resentful at how her chance of happiness had been snatched away by what she saw as an outdated set of rules. The result of Peter's removal to Brussels was that Kensington Palace became a prison where Margaret had to endure her griefs alone, just as her ancestor Queen Anne had endured in that same palace the grief caused by the death of all seventeen of her children.

The key mover in the plan to thwart Margaret's marriage to Peter was the Queen's equerry Alan 'Tommy' Lascelles. Lascelles had also worked for the Queen's father, George VI, and for her uncle, Edward VIII. Lascelles was a dyed-in-the-wool reactionary who felt any relaxation of the old rules would lead to anarchy. Margaret always blamed him for destroying her chance of happiness and this was especially so when her marriage to Antony Armstrong-Jones (later Lord Snowdon, 1930–2017) ended in deep unhappiness. In an act of extraordinary insensitivity, Lascelles was given a grace-and-favour apartment at Kensington after his retirement and he was therefore close to and often seen by the woman whose life he had blighted. On numerous occasions as she was driven out of Kensington Palace, Margaret would catch sight of Lascelles through her car window and curse him. In his 2005 biography of the Queen Mother, Hugo Vickers recalls Margaret shouting to her chauffeur, 'There goes Lascelles. Run the brute down.'

It was after discovering that Peter was about to marry someone else during his time in Brussels that a grief-stricken Margaret determined to lose herself in a new relationship. She fell for Antony Armstrong-Jones despite knowing that he was both extremely promiscuous and bisexual.

As with Margaret and Peter, so too with Margaret and Tony. Kensington Palace became the stage on which the disaster of their extraordinary marriage was played out. Margaret was drawn to Tony because he was unconventional, but it was this very unconventionality that destroyed their marriage. From day one, he was unfaithful to Margaret and she knew it. She came close to having a nervous breakdown soon after the birth of her two children, as he increasingly drifted back to his bohemian life among photographers and models. We know that Tony's studio was a magnet for young women eager to work with a celebrated photographer. Tony, on the other hand, wanted attractive young female assistants largely so he could seduce them. He made sure that no individual assistant stayed long. That meant he could seduce them and quickly move on to the next girl. Simultaneously, he was sleeping with various male friends.

When his growing dislike of his wife reached a particular pitch of unpleasantness, he made a point of sleeping with one or two of her male friends, including two prominent aristocrats who cannot be named as they are still alive and their relationship with Tony has never been publicly acknowledged. What made his promiscuity particularly hard to bear was that he often sneaked his latest lover – whether male or female – into Kensington Palace knowing that Margaret would find out. In conversation with the present author, a friend of the couple recalled how during one bitter row, Margaret screamed at Tony and told him she had just slept with a friend of his. He shot back, 'Don't worry, I slept with him too!'

Having been attracted to Tony because he did not treat her with the sort of insincere deference she was used to as a princess, Margaret found that he was happy to go a step further and treat her with no respect or deference at all.

Like Diana, Princess of Wales, after the collapse of her

marriage to Prince Charles, Margaret retreated; Diana suffered from bulimia and self-harmed, Margaret retreated into a world of alcohol, cigarettes and prescription drugs, including increasingly powerful sedatives.

A member of Margaret's staff recalled finding the princess wandering the corridors at Kensington in a daze, weeping and incoherent with alcohol and drugs. She had to be led back to bed, on the way striking out at a servant because she thought he was her husband. On another occasion staff heard crashing noises and thought Margaret had fallen over – when they reached her sitting room, they found the princess half dressed, drunk and smashing anything she could find that belonged to her husband.

Staff were instructed to keep an eye on her after she was spotted leaving the palace without her security detail and very much the worse for drink. She was pursued and discovered lying asleep just inside the main gates.

Unlike Diana and Charles, Margaret and Tony suffered largely in private, or at least they made no attempt to justify or explain their behaviour to the public. For Margaret, that would have been unthinkable and it may explain why her later pronouncements on the behaviour of both Diana, Princess of Wales, and Sarah, Duchess of York, were so harsh. After the Duchess of York was photographed having her toes sucked by her American boyfriend while she was still married to Prince Andrew, Margaret told her she had brought disgrace on the royal family. According to a palace insider, her letters to Diana, which were equally judgemental, were carefully destroyed because they were so critical of Diana and her attempts to use the media to explain her disastrous relationship with Prince Charles.

A member of the Kensington Palace domestic staff who became quite close to Margaret when she was at her lowest at Kensington remembered how the princess:

> used to ask to see me and would just talk endlessly while asking me if I could do little things for her. Most of her requests were, I thought, just to keep me with her. She had no friends and hated to be alone so even a servant would do – I don't say that to be rude about her; it was just that royals didn't generally behave in this way with staff. She was very lonely and felt trapped because she could not leave the palace as her husband could. He went to and fro as he pleased, but as she was the Queen's sister this was not possible. She used to ask me about my home life just as a distraction from her own woes. I was married then with three children – and she even asked if she might come and have tea with me some time. We both knew this would never happen but I think she fantasised about an ordinary life. Of course, she had no idea what an ordinary life would have been like and she would have hated it really – her problem was that she wanted the impossible: a man who loved her and was attentive, but not a man from her old-fashioned world; she wanted a man who would introduce her to artistic friends who would then welcome and admire her as a fellow artist and not just as a princess. She often said she thought Kensington was a prison and she thought she could have had a career as a singer if she had not been royal, but we both knew it was not as simple as that. She both loved and

hated being a royal and would only have agreed to be a singer if she could have been famous and feted from the start.

Staff were deeply shocked, too, when word spread that Tony seemed to be encouraging his wife to take drugs:

He used to offer her all sorts of drugs in the time before they really fell out – we heard they tried LSD and cocaine, but then a lot of people tried things like that at the time. This was the 1960s and people – even Margaret – tried these things. But in the end when their relationship got really bad, Lord Snowdon used to leave little packets of drugs around their apartment and by Margaret's bed with notes on them saying things such as, 'Why don't you take all these and do us all a favour?' He meant, I think, take so many that you die. He may have been partly joking but he was asking her to commit suicide. We were told to remove any packets we saw and not to mention them to Margaret under any circumstances.

They really used to torture each other you know, but I think with his carefree attitude and freedom from many royal rules he always came out on top. Less was expected of him. When she screamed at him for sleeping with other women, he would wait a few days and then bring one of his young women assistants to the palace and make love noisily to her so Margaret would hear. It was really sadistic, but oddly Margaret only really cared massively when he slept with someone aristocratic. She took the view that sleeping with what she referred to as a 'common tart' was not that worrying – and that infuriated her husband too. But Margaret also slept with people to annoy Tony – she had numerous affairs, including one with a man called John Bindon who had served time in Borstal! She also had a fling with Robin Douglas-Home, a nephew of the Prime Minister Alec Douglas-Home – Robin killed himself after the affair with Margaret ended. And there were lots of others – I remember her being very intimate with a famous pop star, several actors and a politician.

*   *   *

Visitors to Kensington Palace see only the old state rooms – rooms inhabited by William and Mary, Queen Anne, George I and George II. The parts of the palace where Margaret lived, by contrast, were indistinguishable from any modern house owned and designed by wealthy people. She and Tony completely re-designed apartment 1A, ripping out a great deal of the historic fabric, but this was the 1960s and few raised any objections to what might today seem like vandalism. Tony thought of himself as a brilliant interior designer, but all signs of his 1960s interiors at Kensington (they quickly became dated) have long disap-peared. At the time, Princess Margaret was disparaging about what she saw as her husband's over-inflated sense of his own artistic brilliance.

Margaret stayed on at Kensington after her divorce in 1978 and she survived by mixing with people who, deep down, she always feared enjoyed her company only because of who she was. This was Margaret's tragedy, but with the help of travel, drugs, cigarettes and alcohol, she made the best of it for the rest of her life. Befuddled for much of the time, Margaret later watched warily as Charles and Diana married and came to live at Kensington. She knew the dangers of any marriage that brought together two people who were fundamentally unsuited and over the years that followed she saw another royal marriage crash and burn.

* * *

The story of Charles (1948–) and Diana's (1961–97) disastrous relationship is as well known as the story of Margaret and Tony's, but new material is always dripping into the public domain. This is partly due to the fact that Charles and Diana's relationship has been subject to almost endless analysis, but it is also because some of those involved on the edges of the couple's battles – especially Kensington Palace staff and former staff – are now more willing to discuss what they saw and heard.

We know that both before and after Charles and Diana's wedding in 1981 Charles saw his marriage as something he had to do for the family. He was persuaded to marry Diana against his better judgement by his much-loved grandmother whose view of life he had always valued. The Queen Mother and her friend Lady Fermoy, Diana Spencer's grandmother, had decided that Diana was the ideal match for Charles, but unfortunately their views of suitable royal marriages were essentially Victorian. They imagined that Charles and Diana would produce an heir; they imagined that Charles at least would probably want a mistress but that Diana would simply accept this as part of royal life and that she would, if necessary, come to an accommodation with her husband; the idea of divorce would never enter anyone's mind. It was Charles's duty to marry someone suitable and produce an heir and hopefully a spare. This had always been the duty of heirs to the throne and Charles wasn't the first heir to marry someone who would probably never make him happy. Happiness as the primary aim of a marriage would have made no sense to the dynastically minded Queen Mother. Always before her eyes would have been, for example, Charles's great-great-grandfather Edward VII who had married dutifully, sired an heir and then spent his leisure time with a string of mistresses. Edward's wife, Queen Alexandra, was expected to accept this – she was his 'brood mare' – and she would never have dreamed of telling her story to the press or seeking a divorce.

By the time Charles and Diana married and the scandal of their lives together began to unfold, expectations had changed. The Queen Mother and Lady Fermoy hadn't even noticed that the 1960s had ushered in an age when even members of the royal family expected marriage to mean happiness and personal fulfilment. Duty no longer had very much to do with it.

The great risk now of a dangerously unhappy marriage between the heir to the throne and his wife was that the story would get into the newspapers. Gone were the days when the British press refused to print anything unpleasant about the royal family. Newspaper proprietors in the past, most notably Lord Northcliffe and Lord Beaverbrook, forbade their editors to write anything negative about the royal family. They did not want to jeopardise their own invitations to royal events. By the time Charles and Diana's nightmare began, everything had changed and newspaper editors were sharpening their teeth, ready to spring.

Sensitive and in need of a man who would be loyal above all things, Diana was not prepared to be Charles's 'brood mare'.

Both Charles and Diana felt they had a right to personal fulfilment and happiness. The Queen Mother and her daughter Elizabeth II believed happiness was all very well but duty must always come first. A failing marriage must be propped up for the sake of appearances, as the Queen's own marriage to Prince Philip (1921–2021) had been propped up in the 1950s when he is known to have seen other women. But for Charles and Diana this was anathema.

The result was that as Margaret's life at Kensington decayed into a sullen, unhappy quietude, there were new rages to hear and discuss at the old palace. Charles and Diana's rows began almost from day one as they realised – having met only a dozen times before their marriage – that they were almost wholly incompatible. Charles was sensitive and desperately in need of emotional support, but so was Diana. Both were weak and insecure and had endured early lives blighted by poor parenting; both needed a mature, steady partner and Charles already had that in Camilla Parker Bowles (1947–). Diana had no one.

It seems very unlikely that Diana would have strayed into the arms of other men if Charles had been able to give up Camilla. What Camilla had that Diana lacked was not beauty or intelligence, it was maturity and strength.

Camilla's ability to be a substitute mother for Charles was the clincher and it left Diana to spend the rest of her life in search of a similar rock. She described a number of her future lovers as her 'rock', but this was wishful thinking. Like Princess Margaret before her, Diana had a series of boyfriends who never gave her quite what she needed. They were married, like art dealer Oliver Hoare, unreliable, like James Hewitt, or hopelessly immature, like Dodi Fayed.

Faced with the prospect of her husband enjoying life with his mistress while she remained alone, Diana turned to the media to give her a sense of purpose; and something instinctive and largely subconscious in her allowed her to use the media as no one else has ever been able to use it. It is true to say that the tabloids were occasionally cruel to her, but in the main they built her into an icon of compassion, something Meghan Markle would doubtless love to emulate.

Before Diana and then Charles took part in self-justifying television interviews that scandalised the royal family, a great deal was known about just how badly they were getting on. The press had begun to pick up on hints in their unhappy faces and ill-at-ease body language that something was wrong, but at the palace, the staff knew it was already much worse than anyone outside could possibly imagine.

Kitty Power worked for Diana at this time and she explained how Diana was so unhappy at one point that she had begun to self-harm:

I noticed one day that she had these dreadful cut marks on her arm. This was at a time when her bulimia was getting seriously out of control – the smell of vomit in her apartment was over-powering sometimes and her dentist told her that her teeth were being damaged by the acid caused by continual vomiting. But Diana's unhappiness also came out in spectacular rows – mostly she suffered in silence but she was not as timid as people often think. I heard one terrible argument where she threw a heavy ornament at Charles and it smashed a mirror. Charles shouted 'You are insane' or something like that and ran from the room while poor Diana, already in tears shouted, 'You're just a stupid little boy!' Charles always hated confrontation and would usually escape before the storm and he would then write to Diana from Highgrove [House, Charles's grand Georgian mansion in Gloucestershire] trying to persuade her to do what he thought was reasonable – which was to carry on with pretending the marriage was okay and not to complain that he spent most of his time with his mistress. The only time I heard him try to justify what was going on was when he said, 'Look at history – every-one in my position has a mistress. It's just one of those things. I don't mind what you do so long as you do it discreetly. Isn't that enough?'

Diana was a very sweet person in private – she really was what you saw on television. She would apologise to the maids for the mess she made, for example. And often her private apartments were a terrible mess – they reflected her terrible mental state. She was also very good at making you think she took a real interest in you. I lived nearby in a council block in Portobello Road and she actually turned up one afternoon for tea. I was horrified because it was quite a rough estate at that time and she'd walked there on her own! I'd invited her as she had asked if I would, but I never expected she would turn up! My flat was tiny but she never made me feel awkward – in fact I thought she'd never leave! She was actually very good with women because she loved to talk and gossip and I think it was easier for her because she didn't like being an aristocrat. She didn't enjoy the whole royal thing at all. She said she had enjoyed life far more when she was working with small children, which is what she did before the whole Charles thing. She asked me about myself and when I told her I was divorced she asked me how that felt. I made a joke and said that my husband had been horrible so I'd made myself feel better by putting his picture on the wall and throwing darts at it and she said, 'I think I might try that!'

She was under a terrible amount of stress at various times – I noticed for example that she had a habit of twirling her hair constantly in her fingers and it had begun to make a bald spot. She also chewed her lips when she was nervous – sometimes till they bled. I walked her to the Notting Hill end of Portobello Road when she left – she refused to let me walk her back to the palace – and as we crossed the space outside my flats there was a group of small children playing with a ball and she immediately ran across and started playing with them. They just accepted her and for ten minutes her face lit up and she looked genuinely happy throwing the ball and organising the children in a circle. For a few moments she forgot all her troubles – you could see it in her face.

Once Charles and Diana had formally separated and Charles left Kensington Palace for Highgrove, Diana famously threw herself into a string of affairs – lovers were often smuggled into the palace by either Diana herself or domestic staff who had grown close to her and were happy to help, as Kitty Power recalled:

Oh, I helped her on many occasions because it was difficult for her to bring a man into the palace without causing a fuss. If I brought someone in, I would just say he was visiting the princess to discuss some aspect of her work, but I think the security people knew what was really going on because the same person might come three times in a week for a few months or longer before Diana moved on to someone else. And, of course, they usually stayed the night! The thing about Diana was that she was desperately trying to find happiness outside herself – in a man, I mean. She found it impossible to be happy on her own. She once said to me, 'Do you like being alone? I mean do you enjoy it – you know, having time to yourself?' I said I did and she looked very wistfully at me and said, 'You'll have to teach me how to do that. I would love to know.' I think Diana confused sex with love to some extent and because she was very beautiful, men were attracted to her and each time it happened, she felt that the attraction must have more behind it than just sexual desire. I think it was because she always felt warm towards men who wanted her – you have to remember she had grown up in a cold, dysfunctional family. She would fall in love at the drop of a hat. She was deeply in love with both James Hewitt and Oliver Hoare and another man I can't name because he is still alive and married to a distant relative of the Queen.

Stories about Diana's lovers having to hide behind flower pots are legion but one that has not been told before concerned another lover who has never been named. In an interview with the present author a former member of Kensington Palace staff explained that the man in question was a politician, married – unfortunately for Diana – and famously charming:

> When he stayed with Diana at Kensington it often turned into a sort of Brian Rix farce with her friend dashing into the bathroom or hiding behind a curtain every time a member of staff knocked and came into her private rooms. He couldn't understand why Diana was embarrassed that he should be spotted leaving in the morning. And I think his carefree attitude eventually rubbed off on her a bit because she did eventually let him arrive through her front door and she stopped making him hide. To some extent she got her revenge on the family by ceasing to care what people in the palace thought of her and he gave her the strength to do that. But he did get caught once – literally with his trousers down. I don't know how it happened but the staff laughed about it for weeks afterwards. Somehow, he'd got up in the night in his shorts and wandered off until he found a door had closed behind him and he couldn't open it to get back. Diana quickly realised what had happened and went to look for him but he'd been spotted already by a member of staff who just said good morning to him and walked past while he froze, red-faced and trying to pretend nothing was amiss.

Diana's desire to lead a life without the constraints placed on her by the royal family is well known, but as Kitty Power explains:

as she grew in confidence, she tended to ignore the rules more and more. And you would be surprised how different she looked when she dressed up to go out on her own. She used to go out to ring her friends and whichever was her current boyfriend because she was convinced her phone at Kensington was bugged and we all thought it was bugged too – Diana showed me a small device she found stuck underneath her phone. She removed it but a few weeks later there was another one in position! Kensington Palace is a honeycomb of passageways and courtyards so she would go out in different ways and I think the security people on the gate thought she was one of the people from the press office or kitch-en. She liked being naughty too so leaving the palace without permission and in disguise really appealed to her even though she often ended up walking around Kensington on her own and feeling lonely.

But that's just one side of the story. Diana may have had her low points, but she also liked letting go and enjoying herself, as Kitty Power remembered:

She would have quite wild little parties with a few of her friends. She liked to drink a bit as it made her happy and the parties could get a little out of hand – they would throw things out the windows, and she had a sort of pyjama party once with men and women. Next thing we heard they'd got tipsy and run down a corridor with only their pyjama tops on! But this was in the early hours so no one was bothered – except one elderly resident who banged on the walls and shouted for silence! When she was between lovers – which was not usually for long – she would sometimes sleep with a schoolfriend. I remember going into her bedroom one morning and there she was fast asleep and absolutely clinging to her friend!

*   *   *

After the death of Diana in 1997 and Charles's continued residence at Highgrove House, Kensington Palace slumbered on until the arrival of American TV actress Meghan Markle (1981–) following her marriage to Prince Harry (1984–) in 2018.

Royal watchers are always wary of the fairy-tale excitements that surround any and every royal wedding. Previous royal weddings had not always ended well and this one, though it seemed to herald a new modern mixed-race era for the royal family, rang alarm bells from the outset. With Edward VIII always in mind, the court was at best cautiously welcoming of a divorced American. The Queen herself, in a major departure from tradition, made Meghan welcome at numerous events before the marriage. According to insiders, Meghan was also welcomed by Charles who found her delightful and especially by Sophie Wessex, wife of Prince Edward. Sophie had been criticised by the *News of the World* shortly after her marriage to Edward and she tried to help Meghan avoid the obvious pitfalls. With her acting career behind her, Meghan clearly felt that the role of royal princess was one she would be able to play easily. She had, of course, reckoned without the unique nature of the British tabloid press.

There is no doubt press coverage of Meghan did sometimes

border on the racist and in the classic tabloid manner she was built up and praised to the skies and then knocked down and slammed as difficult, demanding and arrogant.

The pressures of negative press stories and difficulties with the rather old-fashioned way in which the royal family works soon led Meghan to feel that her needs were not being met. Staff at Kensington Palace felt that Meghan's complaints about her position in the family were unjustified. She was, they said, rather like someone who joins the army and then wonders why life is so tough. One member of staff insisted that, though Meghan was kind and very friendly, she simply did not understand how different her new world was going to be despite having been coached by Harry, Sophie Wessex and others. Even Meghan later admitted that she had been warned off Harry by friends who said life in the royal family would be very difficult.

Meghan's later claim that she did not even realise, for example, that she would need to curtsey to the Queen every time they met was greeted with derision. The idea that Harry would never have mentioned this seemed to stretch credibility. Meghan certainly hated the lack of freedom at Kensington Palace and was upset because she felt she had changed enough and it was time for the royal family to meet her halfway, something that was never going to happen.

A member of Kensington Palace staff who agreed to speak off the record explained that:

Meghan is so deeply immersed in what we might call 'Californian therapy speak' that she cannot really believe that other people are sincere when they either cannot or will not engage with her on the same level. The idea that the royal family might sit around speaking 'their truths' to each other and talking about working for world compassion is simply naive, but it is what Meghan seems to have expected. Staff didn't believe claims that Harry had not explained to Meghan that the royal family works in a unique way; that it is in fact very much like the army – when you join, you do as the army tells you to do. With his military experience one would have thought that Harry of all people would have explained this to Meghan. But he is so entranced by her that he has completely adopted her way of looking at the world.

After the tough, duty-led stiff upper lip world he grew up in, Meghan's tree-hugging world must have seemed a great relief, but he was foolish to think the royal family would change just because his wife wanted it to be changed.

It is Meghan's vastly different world outlook that led to the most recent royal scandal: the decision of Harry and Meghan to leave the UK for America. It is widely accepted that difficulties with the royal family were an issue here, but that tabloid press coverage was the main driver. There is something odd about this given the numerous savage headlines about the couple in the American media. US headlines have included 'Meghan's Reign of Terror', 'Charles Tells Harry: "Meghan must Go!"', 'Monster Meghan Exposed' and 'Harry Trapped in Marriage from Hell'. If tabloid coverage of the couple really is the main reason they have left for America, they have gone from the frying pan into the fire.

Leaving for America has frightening echoes for the royal family of an earlier exile involving an American woman. It's like a shadowy rerun of Edward VIII leaving the country for love and marriage to Mrs Simpson. When Edward was the Prince of Wales, he hated the stuffy official duties he had to perform, he hated the rigid protocol that surrounded his role and above all he hated the emotionally repressed nature of his family. Escape with Mrs Simpson was his solution. In Harry's case, Meghan represents a similar chance to escape the stiff constraints of royal life and the unemotional nature of his upbringing; Diana's absence from his teenage years and the dreary round of royal duty were always going to be harder to endure for someone who was never going to be king.

But as with Edward there is a price to pay for kicking over the traces and leaving the royal family. Edward was estranged from the family and especially his brother for decades following his abdication; Harry may well find that his estrangement from his brother will last a great deal longer than either would really like. William has clearly accepted the royal family on its terms; he and his future queen give every indication that they will not explain and they will not complain; they have indicated that they will put duty first, but then no doubt Harry and Meghan would argue it is easier for them as their future roles are fixed and immutable. Neither Meghan nor Harry wanted to end up as lost souls, also-rans who eternally play second fiddle to the future king and his wife and family. But there is every danger of that happening anyway, and Meghan's apparent determination to emulate Harry's mother's role as the People's Princess will never change the basic fact that she is married to a man who will never be king.

For the public, too, Meghan's desire to work for world compassion (whatever that is) echoes the kind of thing Diana talked about and many have commented on similarities between Meghan's desire to seem all-caring and all-sharing and Diana's explicitly stated desire to be the Queen of People's Hearts. The British public are far too sceptical to accept – as perhaps the American public would – that an immensely privileged couple should wring their hands about the world's problems while offering only their celebrity status as a solution to those problems. When Meghan and Harry complain on television that they have been cut adrift financially by the royal family, they clearly feel we will be sympathetic. They simply cannot see that it is going to be very hard to sympathise with a couple who have fame, beauty and more than £30 million in the bank yet speak as if they are hard done by and hard up. In the narrow celebrity world they inhabit in California, everyone probably does have more money than they do and it is probably this that makes them lose sight of the fact that there is a vast world out there where people live for a year on what Meghan and Harry might spend in a week.

A member of the Kensington Palace press team at the time Meghan and Harry lived there summed up the perplexity Meghan generated:

She was full of contradictions it seemed to us: she wanted to appear modest, caring and demure in public, but in private she was highly sensitive to anything she felt did not accord her the deference she felt was her due now she was a princess. In this respect she is rather like Princess Margaret. Margaret wanted to be seen as an ordinary person but slapped down anyone who failed to accord her the deference due to a princess. Meghan wants to be seen to be concerned about world poverty but hates it when people ask how an immensely wealthy young woman could know anything about poverty. Meghan loved publicity but felt it was her due always to enjoy positive publicity; when anything negative was published it was always unfair. She was obsessed with this idea of unfairness as if she had never learned that sometimes life is unfair, especially for those whom Meghan wants to help.

Much of the scandal that threatens the royal family as a result of Meghan's unhappiness centres on her absolute refusal to adopt the royal mantra: never complain, never explain. Meghan always insists that she will fight back and win, despite advice that when the British tabloids attack you, it is best to ignore them. If you make a fuss, the press redoubles its efforts to attack.

According to a palace insider:

Meghan had an air about her of always knowing best and if anyone disagreed with her, they were being unreasonable and unfair. Always. In the palace right from the start there was a feeling that Meghan could never fit with the royal family which has what she saw as very old-fashioned ways. Meghan wanted to change the royal family and make them more caring and sharing, happy to sit in a circle and talk about their feelings. When

her ideas were met with incredulity, she could only do one thing
– leave.

As the scandal of Meghan and Harry's escape to America developed, the couple gave an extraordinary TV interview in which they aired their grievances against the British press and the royal family. By arranging to be interviewed by a friend, the chat show host Oprah Winfrey, Meghan ensured that none of her statements were challenged.

*　　*　　*

Research suggests that those under the age of forty tend to see Meghan as badly treated by the royal family and the British press. Those over fifty are far more likely to see Meghan as rich, spoilt, obsessed with her own importance and with a vastly in-flated sense of her own importance in world affairs.

But there is no need to take sides in this. Both views contain elements of truth. Meghan is perhaps both sinned against and sinning. It is true that she genuinely wants to do good in the world even if the British find her 'Californian therapy speak' embarrassing and insincere. It is true that some of the UK media coverage of Meghan was unpleasant and bordering on racist. It is true that many of the attacks on her for being controlling, too full of her own importance and too keen to emulate Princess Diana were unfair.

But it is also true that Meghan is a powerful personality determined to get her way. To use Harry's own phrase, 'What

Meghan wants, Meghan gets.' And Harry should know. Meghan *does* seem to decide to a large extent what she and her husband do and where they go. She *does* believe that the royal family did not give her what she needed and that the family should have listened to her and changed to suit her.

If Meghan really wanted to be a private person, all she needed to do was go back to America and keep quiet. But what Meghan wants is privacy combined with world fame. Meghan insists the UK press was grossly unfair to her; can she really complain if the UK press point out that allowing herself to be interviewed by a good friend is simply going to the other extreme to make sure she gets only the coverage she wants? And the deep dangers can be glimpsed when in the Oprah interview Meghan is encouraged to speak 'her truth'. Well, if we all have our own versions of the truth then there is no truth. Speaking 'my truth' is just a way of ennobling what is after all just one person's opinion.

For the royal family, Meghan and Harry's retreat to America and their decision to use the media to air their complaints about the family has frightening echoes of Charles and Diana turning to television to wash their dirty linen in public.

But Meghan and Harry have gone much further because they exposed themselves to forensic examination. Their complaints are riddled with inconsistencies and absurdities. A *Private Eye* journalist neatly skewered the profound contradictions in the couple's portrait of themselves as victims:

The racism in Britain is so bad we've decided to come to the United States; for security reasons it is better for us to live in a country where everyone has a gun; as an A-list actress I was totally unprepared to enter the media spotlight; as an American actor and friend of Hollywood celebrities I did not have the phone number of a therapist; my letter to my father is deeply private, but Harry's unanswered phone call to his father should be shared with the world; we're broke, apart from the millions Harry's mother left him.

The tragedy of the Meghan and Harry scandal and their increasingly bitter feud with the royal family – a feud that may well turn out to be one of the most damaging in royal history – is that the two sides found it impossible to meet somewhere in the middle. A former member of their public relations team said:

> The royal family *does* change too slowly, but Meghan was trying to force it to change too much and too quickly. Perhaps, too, part of the problem is sheer ignorance. No one at the palace would accept as true Meghan's statement that she had no idea she would need to curtsey to the queen, and yet this is precisely what Meghan told us in her television interview. It seems frankly unbelievable that Meghan did not know that the grandchildren of the monarch who are not in the direct line of succession are not automatically given the title prince, and yet she claimed Archie had been unfairly singled out when he was not made a prince. It's nonsense. It would have taken her two minutes to check.

But the tale of the unhappy royals who made a run for it, who escaped into what they clearly hoped would be the sunlit uplands, is only part of the Meghan and Harry story.

As Meghan and Harry's relationship deepened and became a marriage, the relationship between Harry and his brother, William, deteriorated. As a former Kensington Palace staffer put it:

> There was an almost exact correlation between Harry's growing commitment to Meghan and his growing estrangement from his brother. As he got closer to Meghan, he moved further from William. Before Meghan, William was Harry's oldest and closest friend as well as being his brother. The two had been unusually close for royal brothers, because of the tragedy of their mother's death – a tragedy that occurred when they were both so young – and they really needed each other.
>
> But with William's marriage to Catherine Middleton, Harry was increasingly alone. He still had friends from his clubbing days and from his days in the army, but the loss of his mother when he was still so young left him damaged and in need of someone who could provide the sort of closeness and support that he had once found in his brother.

It is not perhaps going too far to say that like Edward VIII, another vulnerable royal, Harry was always likely to be drawn to a strong, decisive woman. Friends of the couple say that from the very beginning Harry was dazzled not just by Meghan's looks but also by her strength of character and purpose.

The fact that Meghan filled a terrifying gap in Harry's life was all well and good, but after the couple's marriage, Meghan's single-mindedness and desire for change turned a yawning gap between Harry and William into a damaging rift. Where there had simply been space there was now resentment and bafflement. As William and Kate embraced royal duty, Harry and Meghan felt increasingly sidelined. As William and Kate's children were born, Harry slipped further down the line of succession, perhaps exacerbating his sense of being always the spare, never the heir. In offering his full support to Meghan in her struggle to make the royal family change, Harry inevitably became an outsider. Not officially but practically and emotionally and it quickly became inevitable that the feeling of being emotionally distant from his brother would soon develop into a need to be physically distant.

As we have seen, the royal family has survived centuries of crises – but Harry's implicit repudiation of its values is something from which it will not quickly recover.

CHAPTER FIFTEEN

CAR-CRASH ANDY: THE PRINCE AND THE PAEDOPHILE

'Lead me not into temptation; I can find the way myself.'
RITA MAE BROWN

Windsor Castle and the various royal houses on the 4,800-acre Windsor Estate have often been the first port of call for those fleeing unbearable tensions within the royal family. It was to Frogmore Cottage on the estate that Meghan and Harry first retreated from Kensington Palace. It was in Fort Belvedere, also on the estate, that Edward VIII sheltered when he needed to escape the pressures of his hated official role as the Prince of Wales. In more recent times, Windsor was the place in which Her Royal Highness the Queen and her husband Prince Philip settled during the Covid-19 pandemic. But Windsor has also provided a refuge of sorts for the man who is arguably the most scandalous royal of recent times: Prince Andrew, Duke of York (1961–).

The story of Andrew's fall from grace really begins with Ghislaine Maxwell (1961–), youngest child of the disgraced newspaper tycoon Robert Maxwell. Robert, it may be remembered, stole hundreds of millions of pounds from the pension fund of his own newspaper, the *Daily Mirror*. He was a domineering and deeply controlling man who made no secret of the fact that the only one of his children he really loved was Ghislaine. Soon after Robert's death in mysterious circumstances – he fell or was pushed into the sea from his luxury yacht in 1991 – Ghislaine began a relationship with an equally domineering and controlling man: the New York financier Jeffrey Epstein (1953–2019).

By 2008 that relationship had ended, but in that same year Epstein was found guilty of soliciting a minor for prostitution and given an eighteen-month prison sentence. But there was something odd about this sentence because Epstein appears to have been allowed out of prison almost whenever he liked to continue running his businesses. It was the cosy outcome of a plea-bargaining deal by a man with wealthy and influential friends. A wave of further allegations led to Epstein being rearrested in 2019. This time there was no escape: the charges were far more serious and if found guilty Epstein might easily have spent the rest of his life in prison. As it turned out, he was found dead in prison while awaiting trial. By 2020 Ghislaine had also been arrested and charged with procuring underage girls for Epstein, a charge which she denied.

By this time details of Epstein and Ghislaine's web of contacts and friendships were being investigated by journalists in Britain and America. Ghislaine, who was always referred to as a socialite, was extremely well connected and one of her closest friends, it transpired, was Prince Andrew, Duke of York, the third child and second son of Queen Elizabeth II.

Ghislaine had been friends with the prince since university days and it was well known that she had introduced Epstein to him. The three became close and Andrew invited Ghislaine and Epstein to Windsor Castle in 2000 and to Sandringham, where Epstein seems to have taken part in a private pheasant shoot with members of the royal family. Prince Andrew also spent time at Epstein's mansion in New York and at Ghislaine's house in London's Belgravia.

Andrew, Ghislaine and Epstein were clearly good friends but following Epstein's release from prison in 2010, Andrew tried frantically to distance himself from the financier. But it was too late and it is easy to imagine the gasps of horror in royal circles when a young American woman, Virginia Roberts Giuffre, stated under oath that she had been pressured into having sex with Prince Andrew at Ghislaine's Belgravia house when she was just seventeen.

Andrew insisted he had no memory of meeting Ms Roberts, despite the fact that newspapers across the world were able to publish a photograph of Andrew with his arm around a very young-looking Roberts. Friends of the duke tried to suggest that the photograph was a fake but there is no evidence to suggest this is true. Like so many royals who are in trouble, Andrew thought television might be the solution. He chose to meet BBC reporter Emily Maitlis in one of the grand sitting rooms at Buckingham Palace – with its solid, traditional furniture, impressive fireplace and large nineteenth-century painting, the room was no doubt intended to reflect the solid, reliable values of the royal family, but the interview that followed, in which Andrew tried to 'set the record straight' and clear his name, was widely derided as a 'car crash'.

The interview had exactly the opposite effect from the one intended: it made a bad situation much worse. Once again, a younger royal broke the old rule: never complain, never explain. Andrew appeared entitled, arrogant, shifty and uncomfortable. He was vague about his friendship with Epstein – despite film showing him leaving Epstein's New York mansion – and he expressed no sympathy for Epstein's victims. Perhaps the most damaging aspect of the interview was that it revealed how closed off from the world many royals still are.

Prince Andrew's demeanour throughout the interview was curiously detached and many of his claims and explanations were met with incredulity – he said he knew he could not have been with Virginia Roberts Giuffre (then known as Virginia Roberts) on the night in question because he distinctly remembered dining at a branch of Pizza Express. He said that the famous photograph of him with Roberts was suspicious because in it he was sweating and, following an adrenalin overload during the Falklands War, he was in fact unable to sweat.

The ultimate absurdity came in the line: 'I admit fully my judgement was probably coloured by my tendency to be too honourable but that's just the way it is.'

Andrew's belief in himself continued after the interview. He was in high spirits thinking it had gone well and that it would entirely clear the air. In fact, he was so pleased with himself that he gave Maitlis an impromptu tour of the palace.

When the response to the interview became clear, the royal family and the royal PR machine went into overdrive. The Queen issued a statement to the effect that Andrew – her favourite son – would no longer represent the royal family. All his royal duties came to an end and all his honorary titles were taken away. As a working royal he had ceased to exist.

Andrew quickly retreated to Royal Lodge, Windsor, where he has remained. He is rarely seen and attends no functions. Bizarrely, he is now living again with his ex-wife, Sarah, Duchess of York, herself no stranger to scandal. We may recall the 1992 incident in which she was photographed having her toes sucked by her American lover (while still married to Andrew) or the occasion on which she was secretly filmed trying to sell access to her ex-husband for half a million pounds. On the grounds of their appalling behaviour alone, the Duke and Duchess of York were clearly made for each other.

There is no doubt that 'Randy Andy' – a nickname that has dogged him for much of his adult life – would have travelled much further into exile than Windsor if that had been possible. Of course, America was always out of the question, despite the presence there of his nephew Prince Harry, because there is every chance that, were he to set foot in the United States, he would be arrested. And that would be a royal scandal to end all royal scandals!

EPILOGUE

Let loose at last from the restrictions of ancient rules, members of the royal family may divorce, may marry divorcees and commoners and may marry people of mixed race and this is all to the good. In the past, the monarchy believed at times that its role was to uphold moral values so that the rest of the population might look up to them and hope to emulate their behaviour. That idea is now dead and the royal family's aim, if it can be said to have an aim, is to reflect the values of modern British society; to be tolerant of people of all creeds and colours; to accept that relationships do break down and people do behave badly and get divorced. If royal scandals have had one great positive effect it is that they have made us see that members of a once absurdly elevated institution are really just fallible human beings like the rest of us.

Of course, there is a downside to all this. If kings and queens are in the process of losing the special magic that once came with royalty, there is a danger that we may come to wonder why we need a royal family at all.

During a trip to Canada, Prince Philip said, 'If at any stage people feel that the monarchy has no further part to play, then for goodness' sake let's end the thing on amicable terms.' In a brief conversation with the present author, Philip went further and said, 'If we're no bloody good, get rid of us!'

As we have seen in this book, it is impossible to imagine Edward II or James I or even that great libertine Charles I saying something like this. In the past the magic of royalty had less to do with serving the nation – the idea behind Prince Philip's outburst – and far more to do with the mystical idea that monarchs were God's anointed on Earth, an idea that has vanished completely.

The great shift in attitudes towards the royal family and our willingness to judge them came after the First World War when across Europe monarchs were toppled and royal houses vanished.

George V rode home on the last vestiges of ancient deference but to a large extent he was well behaved if dull. However, the abdication of Edward VIII followed by the huge shift in social values in the 1960s changed everything and royalty became the plaything of the press – its members criticised, mocked and occasionally praised, but all signs of ancient deference gone. As we have seen, the royal scandals of the past fifty years and more have increasingly played out in public.

But if lèse-majesté has gone, there is no sign that we are ready to abolish royalty. The United Kingdom is one of the last few countries in Europe to retain its royal family, in part, at least, because it gives us a special group of celebrities about whom we can gossip and speculate. The fact that we are continually fascinated by members of the royal family, and especially when they behave scandalously, may well be the very thing that helps the institution to survive. Why would we remove something that adds to the gaiety of the nation?

And even if we were to take that final step and abolish the monarchy, many of the palaces and houses in which the royals' extraordinary lives played out over the centuries would remain. The glittering residences where royals lied and cheated, slept with other people's wives or entertained their mistresses and boyfriends would still be there; ghostly reminders of centuries of royals behaving badly.

BIBLIOGRAPHY

Ackroyd, Peter, *London: The Biography* (Chatto & Windus, 2000)

Ackroyd, Peter, *Revolution: A History of England Volume IV* (Pan, 2017)

Adlard, John, ed., *The Debt to Pleasure: John Wilmot, Earl of Rochester, in the Eyes of His Contemporaries and in His Own Poetry and Prose* (Carcanet Press, 1974)

Allen, Robert C., *Enclosure and the Yeoman: The Agricultural Development of the South Midlands 1450–1850* (Clarendon Press, 1992)

Appleyard, J., *William of Orange and the English Revolution* (J. M. Dent, 1908)

Aronson, Theo, *Prince Eddy and the Homosexual Underworld* (Lume Books, 2020)

Bagehot, Walter, *The British Constitution*, ed. Paul Smith (Cambridge University Press, 2001)

Bain, Joseph, ed., *The Border Papers: Calendar of Letters and Papers Relating to the Affairs of the Borders of England and Scotland*, vols 1–2 (Edinburgh, 1894–96)

Bain, Joseph, ed., *Calendar of the State Papers Relating to Scotland and Mary, Queen of Scots, 1547–1603* (Edinburgh, 1898–1969)

Baker, Richard, *A Chronicle of the Kings of England* (London, 1643)

Baldry, A. L., *Royal Palaces*, ed. F. A. Mercer (The Studio, 1935)

Basford, Elisabeth, *Princess Mary: The First Modern Princess* (The History Press, 2021)

Bathurst, Benjamin, ed., *Letters of Two Queens* (Robert Holden & Co., 1924)

Baxter, Stephen, *William III and the Defense of European Liberty, 1650–1702* (Harcourt, Brace & World, 1966)

Beamish, Noel de Vic, *A Royal Scandal: The Story of Sophie Dorothea of Celle, Wife of George I of England* (Robert Hale, 1966)

Bennett, Daphne, *Queen Victoria's Children* (Littlehampton Book Services, 1980)

Berg, Maxine, *Luxury and Pleasure in Eighteenth-Century Britain* (Oxford University Press, 2005)

Bergeron, David, *King James and Letters of Homoerotic Desire* (University of Iowa Press, 1999)

Bloch, Michael, *The Duchess of Windsor* (Weidenfeld & Nicolson, 1996)

Bloch, Michael, *Jeremy Thorpe* (Abacus Books, 2016)

Boswell, James, *Boswell's London Journal, 1762–63*, ed. Frederick A. Pottle (William Heinemann, 1950)

Bowack, John, *The Antiquities of Middlesex* (W. Redmayne, 1705)

Brown, Craig, *Ma'am Darling: 99 Glimpses of Princess Margaret* (Fourth Estate, 2017)

Bryant, Chris, *Entitled: A Critical History of the British Aristocracy* (Doubleday, 2017)

Bunbury, Henry, *A Narrative of the Campaign in North Holland, 1799* (T. & W. Boone, 1849)

Burnet, Bishop Gilbert, *History of His Own Time* (William Smith, 1838)

Carter, Miranda, *Anthony Blunt: His Lives* (Pan, 2002)

Castiglione, Baldassare, *The Book of the Courtier*, trans. Thomas Hoby (J. M. Dent, 1974)

Chandler, Glenn, *The Sins of Jack Saul: The True Story of Dublin Jack and the Cleveland Street Scandal* (Grosvenor House Publishing, 2016)

Channon, Henry, *Chips: The Diaries of Sir Henry Channon* (Weidenfeld & Nicolson, 1993)

Charlton, John, *Kensington Palace: An Illustrated Guide to the State Apartments* (HMSO, 1958)

Cherry, B. and Pevsner, N., *The Buildings of England, London 3: North West* (Penguin, 1991)

Claydon, Tony and Speck, W. A., *William and Mary* (Oxford University Press, 2007)

Cook, Andrew, *Prince Eddy: The King Britain Never Had* (The History Press, 2011)

Curzon, Catherine, *Life in the Georgian Court* (Pen & Sword History, 2016)

Davies, Philip, *Lost London, 1870–1945* (Transatlantic Press, 2009)

Dempster, Nigel and Evans, Peter, *Behind Palace Doors* (Orion, 1993)

Dennison, Matthew, *Queen Victoria: A Life of Contradictions* (William Collins, 2013)

Dobson, Austin, *Old Kensington Palace and Other Papers* (Humphrey Milford, 1926)

Faulkner, Thomas, *History and Antiquities of Kensington* (T. Egerton, 1820)

Field, Ophelia, *The Favourite: Sarah, Duchess of Marlborough* (Hodder & Stoughton, 2002)

Finch, Barbara Clay, *Lives of the Princesses of Wales* (Remington and Co., 1883)

Flanders, Judith, *Consuming Passions: Leisure and Pleasure in Victorian Britain* (HarperPress, 2006)

French, George Russell, *The Ancestry of Her Majesty Queen Victoria and His Royal Highness Prince Albert* (William Pickering, 1841)

Fryman, Olivia, ed., *Kensington Palace: Art, Architecture and Society* (Yale University Press, 2018)

Fulford, Roger, *The Wicked Uncles: The Father of Queen Victoria and His Brothers* (Arno, 1968)

Glasheen, Joan, *The Secret People of the Palaces: The Royal Household from the Plantagenets to Queen Victoria* (Batsford, 1998)

Graham, Eleanor, *The Making of a Queen: Victoria at Kensington Palace* (J. Cape, 1940)

Greig, Hannah, *The Beau Monde: Fashionable Society in Georgian London* (Oxford University Press, 2013)

Guisborough, Walter of, *The Chronicle of Walter of Guisborough*, ed. Harry Rothwell (Royal Historical Society, 1957)

Hadlow, Janice, *The Strangest Family: The Private Lives of George III, Queen Charlotte and the Hanoverians* (William Collins, 2014)

Haley, K. H. D., *William of Orange and the English Opposition, 1672–4* (Clarendon Press, 1953)

Hamilton, Anthony, *Memoirs of the Count de Grammont* (The Bodley Head, 1928)

Harington, John, *The Letters and Epigrams of Sir John Harington*, ed. Norman McClure (University of Philadelphia Press, 1930)

Hatton, Ragnhild, *George I* (Thames & Hudson, 1978)

Hecht, J. Jean, *The Domestic Servant Class in Eighteenth-Century England* (Routledge and Kegan Paul, 1956)

Hervey, John, *Lord Hervey's Memoirs*, ed. Romney Sedgwick (Penguin, 1984)

Hervey, Mary, *Letters of Mary Lepel, Lady Hervey*, ed. John Wilson (BiblioBazaar, 2009)

Hibbert, Christopher, *Edward VII: The Last Victorian King* (Griffin, 2007)

Hoare, Philip, *England's Lost Eden: Adventures in a Victorian Utopia* (Harper Perennial, 2010)

Hoskins, W. G., *The Making of the English Landscape* (Penguin, 1970)

Hunt, Leigh, *The Old Court Suburb* (Hurst and Blackett, 1855)

Impey, Edward, *Kensington Palace: The Official Illustrated History* (Merrell, 2003)

Jackman, Nancy and Quinn, Tom, *The Cook's Tale* (Coronet, 2012)

Jesse, John Heneage, *Memoirs of the Court of England* (Bohn, 1857)

Jordan, Don and Walsh, Michael, *The King's Bed: Ambition and Intimacy in the Court of Charles II* (Pegasus, 2017)

King James VI and I, *Basilikon Doron: Divided into Three Books* (Robert Waldegrave, 1599)

Langford, Paul, *Eighteenth-Century Britain: A Very Short Introduction* (Oxford University Press, 1984)

Lascelles, Alan, *King's Counsellor: Abdication and War: The Diaries of Sir Alan Lascelles*, ed. Duff Hart-Davis (Weidenfeld & Nicolson, 2020)

Law, Ernest, *Kensington Palace: The Birthplace of Queen Victoria* (G. Bell & Sons, 1899)

Leslie, Anita, *Edwardians in Love* (Arrow Books, 1974)

Linebaugh, Peter, *Stop Thief! The Commons, Enclosures, and Resistance* (PM Press, 2014)

Loftie, William John, *Kensington Palace and Gardens* (Farmer & Sons, 1900)

Loftie, William John, *Kensington: Picturesque and Historical* (The Leadenhall Press, 1888)

Lownie, Andrew, *The Mountbattens: Their Lives and Loves* (Blink Publishing, 2020)

Malcolm, James Peller, *Anecdotes of the Manners and Customs of London During the Eighteenth Century* (Longman, Hurst, Rees & Orme, 1810)

Marlowe, Christopher, *Edward II*, ed. Roma Gill (Oxford University Press, 1972)

Marot, Christopher, 'Victoria's Other Self', unpublished PhD (1981)

Melville, Lewis, *Lady Suffolk and Her Circle* (Hutchinson, 1924)

Micheletto, Beatrice Zucca, 'Margaret Hunt, *Women in Eighteenth-Century Europe*', *European History Quarterly*, vol. 45, no. 1 (2015)

Montgomery Hyde, H., *The Cleveland Street Scandal* (W. H. Allen, 1976)

Mortimer, Ian, *The Time Traveller's Guide to Restoration Britain* (Vintage, 2018)

Morton, Andrew, *17 Carnations: The Windsors, The Nazis and The Cover-Up* (Michael O'Mara, 2015)

Morton, Andrew, *Inside Kensington Palace* (Michael O'Mara, 1987)

Mosley, Nicholas, *Beyond the Pale: Sir Oswald Mosley and Family, 1933–80* (Martin Secker & Warburg, 1983)

Murphy, N. T. P., *One Man's London* (Hutchinson, 1989)

Newsome, David, *The Victorian World Picture* (John Murray, 1997)

Pakula, Hannah, *An Uncommon Woman: The Life of Princess Vicky* (Weidenfeld & Nicolson, 2006)

Pasternak, Anna, *Untitled: The Real Wallis Simpson, Duchess of Windsor* (William Collins, 2019)

Pepys, Samuel, *The Diary of Samuel Pepys*, eds Robert Latham and William Matthews (Bell & Hyman, 1985)

Picard, Liza, *Restoration London: Everyday Life in the 1660s* (Weidenfeld & Nicolson, 2004)

Picard, Liza, *Victorian London: The Life of a City 1840–1870* (Weidenfeld & Nicolson, 2006)

Preston, John, *Fall: The Mystery of Robert Maxwell* (Viking, 2021)

Pyne, W. H., *The History of the Royal Residences* (A. Dry, 1819)

Queen Victoria, *Leaves from the Journal of Our Life in the Highlands, from 1848 to 1861* (Smith, Elder & Co., 1868)

Queen Victoria, *The Letters of Queen Victoria*, eds Arthur Christopher Benson and Viscount Esher (John Murray, 1908)

Queen Victoria, *More Leaves from the Journal of Our Life in the Highlands, from 1862 to 1882* (Smith, Elder & Co., 1884)

Quinn, Tom, *Backstairs Billy: The Life of William Tallon* (Biteback Publishing, 2015)

Quinn, Tom, *The Butler's Tale* (Coronet, 2012)

Quinn, Tom, *The Maid's Tale* (Coronet, 2011)

Quinn, Tom, *Mrs Keppel: Mistress to the King* (Biteback Publishing, 2016)

Rait, R. S., *Royal Palaces of England* (Constable & Co., 1911)

Ridley, Jane, *Bertie: A Life of Edward VII* (Chatto & Windus, 2012)

Robertson Scott, J. W., *The Story of the Pall Mall Gazette* (Oxford University Press, 1950)

Rousseau, G. S., *Perilous Enlightenment: Pre- and Post-Modern Discourses: Sexual, Historical* (Manchester University Press, 1991)

Rubin, Miri, *The Hollow Crown: A History of Britain in the Late Middle Ages* (Penguin, 2006)

Russell, Bertrand, *The Autobiography of Bertrand Russell: 1872–1914* (George Allen & Unwin, 1967)

St Aubyn, Giles, *Edward VII: Prince and King* (HarperCollins, 1979)

de Saussure, César-François, *A Foreign View of England in the Reigns of George I and George II*, trans. M. van Muyden (John Murray, 1902)

Sebba, Anne, *That Woman: The Life of Wallis Simpson, Duchess of Windsor* (Phoenix, 2012)

Shaw, Karl, *The Mammoth Book of Oddballs and Eccentrics* (Robinson, 2000)

Simms, R. S., *Kensington Palace* (HMSO, 1934)

Somerset, Anne, *Queen Anne: The Politics of Passion* (HarperPress, 2012)

de Sorbière, Samuel, *A Voyage to England* (J. Woodward, 1709)

Spinks, Stephen, *Edward II the Man: A Doomed Inheritance* (Amberley Publishing, 2019)

Stockmar, Ernst, *Memoirs of Baron Stockmar*, trans. G. A. Müller, ed. F. M. Müller (Longmans, Green & Co., 1872)

Strachey, Lytton, *Eminent Victorians* (Chatto & Windus, 1918)

Strachey, Lytton, *Queen Victoria* (Chatto & Windus, 1921)

Thackeray, William Makepeace, *The Four Georges and the English Humorists* (Alan Sutton, 1995)

Thomas, Keith, *The Ends of Life: Roads to Fulfilment in Early Modern England* (Oxford University Press, 2009)

Thomson, Katherine, *Memoirs of Viscountess Sundon*, vols 1–2 (Henry Colburn, 1847)

Thornbury, Walter, *Old and New London* (Cassell, Petter & Galpin, 1878)

Thorold, Peter, *The London Rich: The Creation of a Great City, from 1666 to the Present* (Viking, 1999)

Tidridge, Nathan, *Prince Edward, Duke of Kent: Father of the Canadian Crown* (Dundurn Press, 2013)

Tinniswood, Adrian, *Behind the Throne: A Domestic History of the Royal Household* (Vintage, 2018)

Tinniswood, Adrian, *His Invention So Fertile: A Life of Sir Christopher Wren* (Jonathan Cape, 2001)

Trethewey, Rachel, *Before Wallis: Edward VIII's Other Women* (The History Press, 2020)

Trevelyan, George Macauley, *The England of Queen Anne* (Longmans, Green & Co., 1932)

Troost, Wout, *William III, The Stadholder-King: A Political Biography* (Routledge, 2005)

Van der Kiste, John, *Queen Victoria's Children* (The History Press, 2009)

Van der Kiste, John, *William and Mary: Heroes of the Glorious Revolution* (The History Press, 2008)

Vansittart, Peter, *London: A Literary Companion* (John Murray, 1992)

Vergil, Polydore, *The Anglica Historia of Polydore Vergil, AD 1485–1537*, trans. and ed. Denys Hays (Royal Historical Society, 1950)

Vickers, Hugo, *Elizabeth, The Queen Mother* (Arrow Books, 2006)

Vickery, Amanda, *Behind Closed Doors: At Home in Georgian England* (Yale University Press, 2009)

Vickery, Amanda, *The Gentleman's Daughter: Women's Lives in Georgian England* (Yale University Press, 1998)

Walpole, Horace, *Reminiscences* (Oxford University Press, 1924)

Warner, Kathryn, *Edward II: The Unconventional King* (Amberley Publishing, 2014)

Warwick, Frances Countess of, *Life's Ebb and Flow* (Hutchinson, 1929)

Weinreb, Ben and Hibbert, Christopher, *The London Encyclopaedia* (Macmillan, 1983)

Weintraub, Stanley, *Albert: Uncrowned King* (John Murray, 1997)

Weintraub, Stanley, *Victoria: Biography of a Queen* (HarperCollins, 1987)

Weir, Alison, *Elizabeth, the Queen* (Vintage, 2009)

Weldon, Anthony, *A Brief History of the Kings of England* (J. Williams, 1766)

Weldon, Anthony, *The Court and Character of King James* (G. Smeeton, 1817)

Wheen, Francis, *The Soul of Indiscretion: Tom Driberg: Poet, Philanderer, Legislator and Outlaw* (Fourth Estate, 2001)

Whitaker-Wilson, Cecil, *Sir Christopher Wren: His Life and Times* (Methuen, 1932)

Williams-Wynn, Frances, *Diaries of a Lady of Quality, from 1797 to 1844*, ed. A. Hayward (Longman, Green, Longman, Roberts & Green, 1864)

Wilmot, John, *The Complete Poems of John Wilmot, Earl of Rochester*, ed. David M. Vieth (Yale University Press, 1968)

Wilson, A. N., *After the Victorians* (Hutchinson, 2005)

Wilson, A. N., *Victoria: A Life* (Atlantic Books, 2014)

Wilson, John, ed., *The Rochester–Savile Letters, 1671–1680* (Ohio State University Press, 1941)

Worsley, Lucy, *Courtiers: The Secret History of Kensington Palace* (Faber & Faber, 2010)